Daddy,

On your retirement

With our fondest love

Sue, John, Alistair
and James.

May 1983.

THE PLEASURES OF FISHING

The
Pleasures
of
Fishing

LOGIE BRUCE LOCKHART

ADAM & CHARLES BLACK
LONDON

FIRST PUBLISHED 1981
A. AND C. BLACK (PUBLISHERS) LIMITED
35 BEDFORD ROW, LONDON WC1R 4JH

© 1981 LOGIE BRUCE LOCKHART

ISBN 0-7136-2136-2

British Library Cataloguing in Publication Data

Lockhart, Logie Bruce
  The pleasures of fishing.
  1. Salmon-fishing   2. Trout fishing
  I. Title
  799.1′755   SH684
  ISBN 0–7136–2136–2

Printed in Great Britain by
Clarke, Doble and Brendon Ltd.,
Plymouth and London.

CONTENTS

Dedication

To my late nephew

KIM BRUCE LOCKHART

Who enjoyed it all so much
and for so short a time.

ACKNOWLEDGEMENTS

The Author would like to thank the following for permission to reprint essays in this book:

Country Life: Silver and Stardust, On the Rocks, The Story to Cap Them All, April Fools in the Boathouse, The Charm of the Hill Lochs, Casting Moss before Carp, By Streams, The Greedy Pike—Fact and Fiction.

Salmon and Trout: The Fish-Loser, Heaven, Hell and Purgatory, Of Burns and Worms, Seals, Sea-Trout and Bladder Wrack, *Vive* Greenwell!, Waders do have their Uses, Dam that Stream.

The Field: The Major's Pool, Putting a Fly over the Germans and the French.

The Scots Magazine: The Call of the Waters.

Eastern Daily Press: In Praise of Schubert.

Angling Times: The Land of the Four Rivers.

Angling: Mighty Preparations.

The Countryman: Boyhood's Lost Freedom.

INTRODUCTION

In this terrible yet marvellous world, some gleams of Heaven irradiate the gloom. I've been lucky enough to enjoy some of the brightest and the best; a close-knit, loving family, more than my fair share of kindnesses received, a capacity for being moved by music (even when played badly by myself), exhilaration, fun and good humoured friends from the worlds of rugby football and squash, a job of consuming interest, and a constitution which has allowed me to enjoy the good things of life.

But none of these has been more faithful a consolation, or so lastingly thrilling an experience as fishing, especially trout fishing, in the loveliest parts of the world. Anglers have their critics: some think them selfish, cruel and lazy. They are accused of escaping from their wives and their work, and of contributing nothing to their society. Perhaps . . . but most anglers care deeply for the environment, and for the balance of nature. They tend to be gentle men, seldom shooting jealous rivals or indulging in violent revolutions, possibly because their wicked passions are diverted to a lesser evil.

Trout fishing may start as a peaceful escape, but it soon reveals itself to be a powerful drug which takes possession of us as an unalterable passion. What youngster who has ever caught a sea trout in a Highland river has ever forgotten the experience? As Winston Churchill said of painting, "It is a joy that accompanies us to the end, or almost to the end of the road".

These reminiscences cover varied moments of comedy and tragedy, exasperation and delight over a period of nearly fifty years. They seek to capture some of the atmosphere of beautiful places from the South of France to the Highlands of Scotland. I hope they will bring back happy memories to my fellow addicts, wherever they may be.

LOGIE BRUCE LOCKHART

Boyhood's Lost Freedom

'Little boys should be seen not heard': how completely that tiresome phrase is misunderstood today! My childhood was vastly more free than that of my children, as my parents' childhood was far more free than mine. Partly, of course, they were the far-off days of middle-class comfort and security in country places: big houses, servants, long holidays, the familiar background of the spoilt and privileged. Partly . . . but not entirely.

From 8.30 am to 5.30 pm, throughout the four long months at home, the grown-ups expected neither to see me nor hear me, to our mutual benefit and joy. I looked forward eagerly to the affectionate reunion with my mother which ended each day, and no less to the occasional expeditions with my busy father. There was an hour of lessons which I actually enjoyed, a bath and light supper with my mother, a bed-time story never skimped or neglected, and prayers. The impression was always conveyed that, whatever strains and crises were going on in the background, the experience was as enjoyable and important to my mother as to me. The creation of this atmosphere depended on the freedom and independence which preceded it. In wet weather a rambling nursery was our kingdom; on fine days, the countryside was our paradise.

There was no fear in those days of violence or of traffic hazards. No-one ever told us, as no-one ever told my parents to 'Come down off the wall', or 'Never talk to strangers' or 'Don't go near the river, dear!' My brothers saw to it that I could swim, my father taught me to fish, I was given all the books about the countryside that the heart could desire, and we learned the rest through our freedom and lively curiosity.

We were given toys, but not expensive ones. Those that gave us lasting pleasure were of our own devising: lino-cutting equipment with its rich smells; a massive old iron spoon to melt down the lead for life preservers and catapult bullets; an improvised mortar made of a drainpipe, which propelled a tennis ball over our three-storey house with the help of a carbide charge sprinkled with water; a land yacht made of soap boxes, pram wheels, curtain rods and sheets, which performed alarmingly in gale conditions; rabbit-coshing by torchlight with golf clubs from the running-board of our ancient car—a blood sport which, however reprehensible, still seems preferable to myxomatosis.

Once or twice a year we went to the Highlands, and there freedom became absolute. Even at the age of eight we were free of restrictions and supervision. I was given a small, black steel rod, tough enough to stand up to every childish form of mishandling, a few lessons on casting and knots, and a limited stock of well-loved flies. Then it was off to the burns or the hill lochs, with no envy for older brothers who might be hiring a boat or a gillie. I had lots of small parr and trout on which to learn, unbelievably beautiful surroundings, and none but the best of companions: herons, dippers and grey wagtails, red deer and even an occasional eagle. There was a kind of fierce joy in the suffering inflicted by the windlashed rain, or, when that died down, by the green-eyed clegs and the midges. Every now and again there was the reward of yellow splash and a solid pull, when some keepable trout at last compensated amply for the tangles, the discomforts and the heartbreak of lost fish.

The impressions gathered before adolescence are said to be of unrepeatable intensity. At the age of six in the magic island of Harris, where the rock pools were so clear that every whisker of a lobster was sharply visible in ten fathoms, I became inescapably fishing mad. While my brothers rowed against the gale blowing down Loch Langabhat, a giant fish seized the fly casually trailed from the rod at the back of the boat beside me. I seized the rod and clasped it to my chest, as my brothers stopped the boat and tried to wrest it from me. In the struggle the fish escaped, and I doubt whether my brothers have yet forgiven me; but that brief frenzy of joy, as I felt the bend of the rod and the tearing of the line and the imminence of battle, outweighed all their angry reproaches.

A year later I was taken to a larger river in Wester Ross. The river swirled round a broad expanse of pebble beach, dry and whitened by the sunlight; beyond the gleaming pebbles was a bank of gorse, so orange deep in colour and heavily perfumed that the scent given off under a hot blue sky after a morning shower was overwhelming. Dreamily I was casting for parr in the runs below the big pool when a flurry of silver and diamonds shattered the quiet ripples. My line cut through the water, my heart jumped even higher than the fish, and I fought and landed my first 1¼lb sea-trout. I clasped the glistening beauty in my arms and stumbled breathlessly to a clearing in the gorse to feast my eyes and soul in ecstasy. Once and for all I knew what Heaven was. Never since have I smelt gorse in high summer without reliving that moment.

I have always been grateful for those years of freedom. What have scholarship, responsibility, duty, hard work or even enjoyable success given to us of comparable value?

The Land of The Four Rivers

> 'But ours the mountain fastness,
> The deep romantic ghylls,
> Where Clough and Dee and Rawthey
> Come singing from the hills'
> *Sedbergh School Song*

Some say that no love is ever again so fierce, all-consuming and true as first love. Being long married, I shall not venture an opinion on this, but I do know that the angler's first river is more hauntingly seductive than any other.

It is not quite true that the Rawthey was my first river; at the age of five I had with wild excitement caught a stickleback in a Warwickshire brook, and over the next few years had glimpsed paradise in some Highland burns and the lochs of the Outer Isles. But it was on the Rawthey, the Clough, the Dee and the Lune, that I served my apprenticeship throughout my teens, and thereafter at intervals through the twenty years my father was Headmaster of Sedbergh.

I was lucky in my tutors. My father had been a boy at Sedbergh and knew the waters well. He was a busy man, and our joint expeditions were rare joys from which I learned a lot. The rest of my teaching was left to long

hours of comparative failure and to Harvey Askew, the
Sedbergh grocer and sometime president of the Angling
Association, a great and kindly little man with a
marvellous accent and, in his advancing years, only one
visible tooth, past which he slipped many a wise
epigram.

The Sedbergh countryside is among the best Britain
can offer, if you do not fear the rain. The Sedbergh
hills—Winder, Higher Winder, and the Calf—are short-
grassed fells, shiny, slippery underfoot, smoothed by
the wind, yellow ochre rather than green. The per-
egrines used to nest on Coombe Scar, and the ravens and
buzzards in Cautley Crags; on Baugh Fell, the grass
turns to heather. It is from these glorious fells that the
four rivers come, and never did rivers more truly sing.

The Clough is a substantial beck, joining the Rawthey
just upstream from Sedbergh; the Dee is a little river
joining it a mile downstream. Three or four miles further
down the Rawthey, swollen by its two tributaries, joins
the better-known Lune in a deep, great, thunderous
pool, full of good but usually inaccessible fish. All of
these rivers flow through barren fell and moorland to
begin with, swift, rocky, cleaner than champagne and
just as bubbly.

As they drop below 500 or 600 feet, they are lined
with trees, and the fishing grows harder as the fish grow
more keepable. The Clough comes from the land of
limestone caves and, after Danny Bridge, is small and
overhung; a succession of little waterfalls over shelving
rock, interspaced with pools 3ft or 4ft deep.

The Dee, flowing down from Dent, is less hurried,
wider and full of twinkling, pebbly runs, which are
neither pool nor rapid. The Rawthey, twice as big, is as
varied as a Northern trout stream can be. In spate it can

be fierce and frightening, rising as abruptly as the Findhorn and changing colour swiftly from that of mild beer to not-so-white coffee. Its banks vary from bleached pebble beaches to grassy paths, from sand-banks to flat rocks and huge boulders. It flows through bogland, heather, oak woods, pine woods, and meadows thick with buttercups. There are great deep rock pools like Lord's Dub (a bather's heaven), raging rapids, elegant runs, and charming backwaters. The lovely pool where Dee meets Rawthey is linked with Water's Meet of Rawthey and Lune by four miles of river that visually is sheer delight.

For years I thrashed these rivers, as I had been taught to fish Highland rivers, wet fly, across and downstream. In holiday time I fished from morning until night. I caught multitudes of parr and did little execution among the trout except when the water was coloured. On bright days I was reduced to fishing for eels over Millthrop bridge, with worms. I watched with fury as a a boy called Kelsall (who later became, I believe, fishery officer for Lake Victoria) brought back plenty of trout of up to a pound or more from the Clough, where I caught nothing. I was even more resentful when a Borderer by the name of Charlie Douglas brought back even larger ones by tickling them or by using a noose.

Kelsall used a small spinner, fishing upstream with a short line and supreme dexterity. I still feel it was murder. I doubt I would have survived the discourage-ment of those long hours of fruitless hard labour if it had not been for the glory of the riverside dappled with sunlight and flowers, alive with dippers, sandpipers, grey wagtails and oystercatchers.

Then I began to take advice. I changed to upstream wet fly, and I began to note carefully the time of the rises at different times of the year and in different weather. Success came. Over the breathless excitement of stealthy wading, stalking my fish with a very short line and straining to keep my body bent low over the water, the long hours of failure were forgotten, and I began to know all the best lies and to catch the good fish.

Partridge and Orange, Snipe and Purple, and March Brown, became my trusted friends. I never tried the stone fly beloved of the locals, nor dry fly, a skill I acquired later in the South, and which no-one ever appeared to try on those waters. Looking back on it, and remembering the success of dry fly on the Tweed, I can only think it would have been highly successful.

It was a good day if the trout averaged ¾lb—but it was always exciting. There were some big ones, and I remember one of 1lb 14oz in splendid condition which gave me a great fight in rough water. Although we never went after the sea-trout exclusively (they were mostly caught by night-fishing and were less common on the Rawthey than in the Lune), there was always a chance, and I collected one or two over the years. My brother, far less assiduous, landed a 7lb salmon on a small March Brown and 3x gut.

The evening rise in July could be dramatic, and there were backwaters where the best trout would dimple away within inches of the bank and would bravely take a well-presented upstream wet fly in almost still water.

Late evening or night-fishing on the Lune with Harvey Askew was always an adventure. There was a black velvet hush, when the softest cast in the deeper, slower pools would catch the moon or starlight and lay a silver track across the unbroken dark of the suface. The rise of a sea-trout in such circumstances was a shattering explosion which would set my heart thumping. It was a stiff examination in fishing efficiency . . . one could not run the risk of a tangle or of catching an overhanging branch.

One such night, just at sunset, I was astonished to see a huge head and tail rise about ten yards upstream of me. I kept still and, like a playful seal, a large otter swam past me downstream; surfacing so close to me that I could have hit him on the head with my rod.

Sedbergh has not changed much. The stocks were diminished in war time by some surreptitious use of grenades, and there was always a deal of poaching for salmon as well as trout. The rivers are no doubt more heavily fished now, but there is no likelihood of pollution, and the tourists still pass them by. These are waters that need knowing and loving, and that is their best insurance. Long may it remain so.

The Story to Cap Them All

Mighty are his preparations. He goeth forth early in the morning and cometh home late at night, smelling of strong drink . . . and lo! The truth is not in him!

Although he was never averse to a dram, I would not go as far as to accuse my Uncle B. of being That Kind of Angler. After all, he achieved fame: a knighthood, an expert knowledge of Eastern Europe and authorship of some charming books, including one on fishing, from whose pages of pleasing blarney modest flashes of veracity occasionally peep out. *My Rod, My Comfort* is not a boastful book, but it seems strange to me that, although Uncle B. was to my certain knowledge a participant in one of the most remarkable fishing stories of all time, it does not, as far as I know, figure in any of his reminiscences. My sources are unimpeachable, for the other participant was my father, who was constitutionally incapable of giving himself the benefit of the smallest exaggeration over a span of thirty years, let alone of inventing a tale so improbable as to defy belief.

It all happened before the second world war, and certainly long before Uncle B. devoted himself to a programme of research for his celebrated book on Scotch.

Ravenglass was then one of those Midland reservoirs which, when new, gained a bubble reputation for growth rate. It had been going for a few years, and certainly contained some monstrous trout. Uncle B. was staying with my father at a time when the latter was a Housemaster at Rugby School. During one of their rare get-togethers, they determined to escape for a day to the new reservoir. They went off with high expectations and heads buzzing with reminiscences of their happy childhood expeditions on Speyside. Their friendship however, was more competitive than loquacious and they determined to take a boat each, so as to explore the water more thoroughly and to set about their rivalry in their own way. They agreed to meet for lunch, to compare notes and to part again until after the evening rise.

New reservoirs are notoriously tricky. For a season or two the fish are fat, hard fighting, greedy and naïve. Soon, however, they grow sulky and unpredictable. The big ones turn to bottom feeding or become cannibals, until anglers are reduced to sink and draw techniques with lures, which are really no more than disguised minnows rather than genuine flies. It is a poor kind of sport, and my father and Uncle B. would not stoop to anything but orthodox wet flies. On a day when nothing seemed to be rising to surface flies, it is not surprising that they both had a bad morning. My father had at last struck one very large fish which came to his tail fly, but to his chagrin, it had broken him and carried away his whole cast.

They munched their way through a gloomy lunch and parted, hoping for better things in the afternoon. The conditions went from bad to worse. The wind dropped, the sun came out, and the trout sulked. It even got beyond the stage of ripple chasing: not a rise dimpled the mirror surface. They flogged the lake, often half a mile apart, with that resigned stoicism which is the mark of determined Scottish anglers who have lost all hope but have paid their whack. My father never saw another fish, but just before he had made up his mind to return to the shore, he heard a bellow of triumph and excitement from his brother, saw a mightily bent rod and a tremendous prolonged struggle with much rocking of the boat, splashing and oaths.

When they met on shore Uncle B. held up two trout. I can no longer safely record their weight, but both were certainly well over 2lbs each. He also held up—no doubt you've guessed it—my father's cast. But he hadn't hooked the fish which had broken my father, or, indeed, the other fish. His tail fly had hooked the cast, which must have been pulled taut between the two trout. After father's original fish had taken the tail fly and broken the cast, another must have seized the dropper which was trailing from the first fish's mouth. Uncle B. had by pure chance hooked the gut between them, and played them see-saw fashion with the cast sliding along the hook of his own fly. How the tackle stood up to the strain we shall never know, and what the odds against the repetition of such a coincidence must be in a lake of that large size, I leave it to statisticians to calculate. Although the playing of two such substantial fish must, under the circumstances, have called for rare skill and judgment, even Uncle B. would not have claimed that his success on that occasion owed nothing to luck.

The Fish-Loser

Perhaps it is a form of masochism born of incipient senility, but I have come to believe that I actually enjoy losing fish.

When very small, I made a spectacular start on my fish-losing career. The senior members of the family were fishing in Loch Mudle from the safe comfort of a boat; I had been dismissed to the burn.

Suddenly a swirl like a seal at play sent my heart plunging through my stomach. I struck wildly, and a great fish steamed down the swollen burn with small boy in pursuit. At the age of eight I had no clear standard of comparison, but I knew this was no ordinary burn sea-trout. With helpless desperation I hung on while the salmon did what it liked.

Fortunately, there were no trees along the bank, no waterfalls or rapids, and I was able to prevent him taking out all the line by running after him. How that fish didn't break me I shall never know: but after what seemed an eternity, it lay below me, tired and almost motionless, within reach of my net. The burn was deep, and the heather hung far out over the bank. The net was tiny, little more than a toy. It was all I could do to reach the giant fish at full stretch without falling through the heather into six feet of water.

He was too big for the net, but I did get his tail end in, and for a moment he was balanced in mid air on his way to the bank. But his unexpected weight, once out of the water, was too much for me. The net wobbled, he gave a last flop, and I saw—and even heard—the gut snap just above the fly.

He lay there stunned for a second, and I could see the gleam of the Mallard and Silver in his upper jaw. Without waiting to think, splash! I threw down rod and net and jumped straight on top of him. The water was well out of my depth but that didn't matter, because I felt him in my arms for a fraction of a second before he escaped with a wriggle and a flap. That feeling will be with me to my dying day. As I kicked my way to the surface I saw a great wave as he sped through the shallows at the head of the pool, and away . . .

No-one but a born fisherman can understand the agony of that moment. I wept, and for years afterwards the pain returned whenever I thought of it. There had been no witnesses; the memory had to remain an unshared secret.

Over the years, I have lost a great many more fish. Habit has dulled the pain. Grown-ups don't weep. 'I accept the universe!' said some gushing lady to Thomas Carlyle. 'Gad! You'd better!' was his sardonic reply. These words have inspired me to look back at all the fish I've lost in a new way. How much happier a place the world must be for all those prize trout still at large! One remembers all the fish one loses, not many of those one catches. How rich in such memories I have become! While others point to desiccated specimens of such and such a weight, caught in such and such a place on a given date, growing dusty in glass cases on the unlit side of the front hall, mine lurk alive and still growing, monstrous shadowy forms forever haunting the deep waters of my vivid memory.

Now, like many middle-aged fishermen, I've philosophised my way to an almost oriental patient-at-oneness with the will of the wind and the waters. When I first took my sons down to the Tweed, my heart beat wildly to see the primeval emotions flitting across their faces as failure and success followed one another in their eternally unjust and erratic way. I have to recognise that my role is now that of the elder statesman, counselling patience and calm in every adversity. I've fished that water for thirty years; I've hooked and lost salmon on my trout rod. It has nothing worse in store, no new horror to sear my battle-scarred soul.

On the Saturday of the Melrose seven-a-sides, which I should have been watching, I went down to Lord Haig's stretch with my son, Bede. It is lovely water with a stately salmon pool below a wooded bank spattered with primroses. Up and downstream, the broad Tweed curves its way at the bottom of a 300ft valley with sides which defy access. How beautiful the April waters on this sparkling day, and how misleading. The wading is difficult and treacherous at the Gate Heugh above 400 yards of tumbling trout runs.

In low water the depth varies from 1½–3ft with a narrow channel for the mainstream some 3ft deeper; an ideal succession of half-pools and half-rapids. Given a heavy shower, the river rises rapidly by a further dangerous 2ft. The bottom consists of a blend of large slippery boulders and shelving rocks, which can plunge one over the top of one's waders into the powerful currrent at any time. We fished our way up this formidable stretch with toil and tribulation. Few trout were showing, although we had seen an 11lb salmon landed. I had two small trout and a grayling, and Bede, cold and wet after two blank and unlucky days, was on the point of giving up in despair.

At the top of the Gate Heugh is a big flat rock; casting upstream from it, I have caught many a good trout, including my best-ever Tweed brown trout of 1lb 14oz. Cold and tired, I had just concluded that no more trout would be rising for it was past three o'clock. Nevertheless, the rock offered comparative comfort, and I continued for a few moments, and was encouraged by rising and missing a good fish. There was a promising-looking eddy a little further out, so I ventured out from the rock into the deeper water, and on a long line rose and this time hooked another.

To my surprise it tore my line out upstream in the irresistible way which announces something really substantial. Instead of stopping after the first surge, it went on. I held on nervously as my little 8ft rod bent alarmingly, and remembered that it was last year's nylon, and 4lb breaking strain at that. What sort of hold had my tiny Greenwell got? The fish leaped, silhouetted against the dancing, dazzling sunlit ripples. It was big, but I couldn't see it clearly, it looked too dark for a grilse or a sea-trout.

There followed a grim battle as the fish swung round me in a semi-circle, boring deep. I tried to recover line, and it came to within a few feet. I fumbled at my net, but my best efforts to hold against the current failed, and it took out more line, until it was far below me, and I wondered whether I could ever stop it. For a long time there was deadlock, but eventually I got some line back and saw him come up to the surface with a great back fin. Clearly he was a brown trout, but I could not guess the size except to say that he was certainly over 4lbs, and the hardest-fighting trout I had ever felt.

I brought him almost within netting range again, but he was plainly just resting, for he swirled to the top, jumped again, making my rod rattle, and made off downstream like a marlin. By this time, Bede, who had seen the fight from far below, was struggling up to see the fun. Despairing of ever forcing the fish up against the current and not daring to make for the bank, because the perilous wading might make me stumble and fall, I remained uneasily perched on top of a vast submarine boulder, praying I should not lose my balance. Slowly I coaxed him round to the inshore side of me, hoping that Bede, twenty yards below me, might be able to net him in the quieter and shallower waters.

I had always believed there were giant trout in the Gate Heugh and now I would be able to prove it. I briefly visualised whether this one would look better in a glass case in the entrance hall or the drawing room. But now the devil must have entered into him, for suddenly, he was away again. His strength took me aback, the rod bent to a croquet hoop as the fish made straight for Bede, who wisely resisted having a dab with the net as the line actually brushed against his waders.

I nearly lost my foothold, got my balance again and tried to slow the fish, only to be encountered by a final burst of power—and he was away! The fly had gone with him and the line flapped loose. All philosophy forgotten, I swore and bellowed, and even thrashed the river with my impotent and fly-less cast, like John Cleese thrashing his car for stalling. In my fury I actually jumped up and down like a naughty child, staggered, slipped over the top of my waders, and wrenched my arm in my attempt to recover. All the accumulated misery of every fish ever lost came back multiplied a hundred-fold as I cursed the river, the sport and the futility of life.

With a final bellow of pain and anger, I looked towards my son for sympathy.

He was roaring with laughter.

Mighty Preparations!

It always was a mistake to believe that fishing, especially trout fishing, called for patience. It is, of course, a fever, an all-consuming lust that can brook neither opposition nor interruption. There comes a day, in late April or early May, when the breeze veers to the south-west, and the call of the river rises to an irresistible crescendo. For some of us it is the water itself that calls, the dancing of the ripples in the bright sun, which suddenly heats the anorak between our shoulder blades with all the tingling hope of a new season. For others it is the ardent worship of Spring's return to the river banks; or the deep urge for the hunt, the cunning pursuit, the delicacy of casting, the excitement of the rise, the fight and the capture, or the splendour of the trout's colours and texture fresh and gleaming in the water. Even in middle age, when in the distance I first see the river at the beginning of another year, I break into a run and am overcome with clumsiness in my impatience to get started.

For others, especially in old age, this impatient lust is replaced by a steadier passion. Like true gourmets they derive their highest pleasures as much from anticipation as from action. The lucky ones among them have more time and money. The fever is not just focused on the fishing itself, but is spread for hours, days or weeks over the preparations for the final assault. The first crocus which opens to the February sun sends them scurrying to their fishing bags. They try their lines to hear the purring of the reel evoke the excitements of past seasons. They fuss around inspecting the joints of their rods, checking the hooks of their flies for rust; they re-grease the dry fly line and rearrange their old favourites: Greenwell, Wickham, Tupp, Blue Dun, March Brown. Every good fisherman must see that his equipment is in good order; and he is never at a loss for an excuse for finding time to adjust, improve and repair, working away in a trance of bliss.

The modern fisherman's eagerness for fiddling with his equipment, however, is insignificant compared to the intense zest and thoroughness of our forefathers. They lived in more leisured times and angling equipment was not mass produced. There were no limits to the care, time and money they devoted to their mighty preparations. Not only did they make their own rods, lines, casts and flies with a skill and originality far beyond our dreams, but each fisherman invested his creations with an individual brand of magic: hocus-pocus formulae for success in which they had complete faith.

Merely in order to anoint his bait and invest it with unique attractiveness, Thomas Best in the *Art of Angling* recommends the

> ne plus ultra of all these kinds of ointments, composed by M. Charras, apothecary royal to Louis the Fourteenth . . . Take cat's fat, heron's fat and the best assafoetida, of each two drachms, mummy, finely powdered, ditto, cummin seed, finely powdered, two scruples, and camphoe, galbanum, and Venice turpentine, of each one drachm, and civet, two grains. Make them secundum artem, into a

thinnish ointment, with the chemical oils of lavender, anniseed and camomile, and keep it in a narrow mouthed well glazed gallipot, covered with a bladder and leather, and it will keep two years . . . anoint your bait with it, and about eight or nine inches of line . . . probatum est!

Then, as now, it was the specialist carp fishermen whose preparations were the most extreme. H. T. Sheringham, in his book on coarse fishing, was not talking of war time when he wrote

> You cannot, of course, fish for big carp in half a day. It takes a month . . . in the first week, having made ready your tackle and plumbed the depths, you build yourself a wattled screen, behind which you may take cover. By the second week the fish should have grown accustomed to this and you begin to throw in the ground-bait composed of bread, bran, biscuits, peas, beans, strawberries, rice, pearl barley, aniseed cake, worms, banana and potato . . . This ground baiting must not be overdone [!] . . . With the fourth week comes the critical time . . . on Monday you leave your rod on the wattled fence so that its top projects eighteen inches over the water. On Tuesday you creep up and push it gently, so that the 18″ become four feet . . . On Wednesday, Thursday and Friday you employ the final and great ruse. This is to place your line . . . gently in the water, the bullet just touching the bottom so that the float cocks, and the two feet of gut which lie on the bottom beyond it terminating with a bait in which is no fraudulent hook. And at last on Saturday . . .

he fishes for and loses his carp!

If it took them a month to stalk one specimen, it is no wonder that the anglers of old took such trouble over their preparation of carp for the table. James Chetham in *The Anglers' Vade Mecum* explains why carp was so great a delicacy but at the same time he shows us why it hasn't really caught on in our time.

> Take a Carp (alive if possible) scour him and rub him clean with water and salt . . . then open him, and put him with his blood and his liver into a small pot then take sweet Marjoram, Thyme and Parsley, of each half a handful, a Sprig of Rosemary, and another of Savory, bind them into two or three bundles, and put them to your Carp, with four of five whole onions, twenty pickled oysters, and three anchovies. Then pour upon your Carp as much Claret wine as will cover him, and season your Claret with Salt, Cloves, Mace, sliced Nutmegs and the rinds of Oranges and Lemons; that done, cover your pot, and set it over a quick fire, till it be sufficiently boiled; then take out the Carp, and lay it with the Broth in the Dish, and pour upon it a quarter of a pound of the best fresh Butter melted and beaten with a half a dozen spoonfuls of the Broth, the Yolks of two or three Eggs, and some of the Herbs shred; garnishing your dish with Lemons, and so serve it up, and you'll find it a noble Dish.

Spacious days, indeed, and mighty preparations. But I still don't like carp!

Silver and Stardust

Life is getting harder for the sea-trout fishermen. As tarmac surfaces are opening up the Highlands and Islands, the big rivers and the best-known lochs are becoming more and more expensive. In order to escape the commercial beat, the faithful few, whose forefathers braved Glencoe annually in the days when the Old Road presented a real challenge, are being driven to the limit of their ingenuity. The most knowledgeable ones can still find a few remote burns and inaccessible lochs. In the meantime Glencoe in August is as populated as Hampstead Heath on a bank holiday. The famous waters of the north-west are being taken over by a new race: the grim-faced hardware-mongers from the south who pay their money, throw in their efficient machinery and recover as much cash in salmon flesh as they can. Most of them seem to care little for beauty or solitude; many would not know the difference between a raven or a rook, or a red-throated diver and a mallard.

Fortunately even when the Highlands have been turned into a glorified scout camp, there will remain a few hill lochs and trackless wastes, to which the new race of fishermen will never attain. Weak knees will not force a way through the clinging bracken and heather, and white flesh will always be succulently vulnerable to that most faithful defender of the wilderness; the midge. There will always be a majority of mankind who actually prefer Margate beach to a rainstorm 1000 feet up in the Western Highlands. But in the case of sea-trout the remote fastnesses are rare; there is a limit to the rapids and falls they can negotiate. Small wonder that the sea-trout fisherman is being driven to explore the sea itself.

Whatever else is scarce in Scotland there is an abundance of coastline. If the entire population of Britain were distributed round the shores of the lochs and islands there would be plenty of space between. And fishing in the salt sea from the shore is every man's right. It is often said that some lochs are only worth fishing in exceptional conditions, and even then only near the mouth of a river, but I have my doubts.

One day I was pondering these problems on the shore of Loch Linnhe, in Argyllshire, at least four miles from the nearest burn. It was a pleasant afternoon, and to while away the time I set to practising casting between the floating patches of seaweed. After the usual couple of little copper-coloured saithe, there was a flash of white, and I was delighted to hook and land a sizeable finnock which gave a lot of fun on an 8ft 6in. trout rod among slippery rocks and a forest of bladder wrack.

Encouraged by this, I camped for the next night by another sea loch a few hundred yards from the mouth of a burn. At first light I peered out at the water. The morning was grey, and relatively still, but some sea-trout were to be seen splashing quite close in. I slithered down on weed-clad rocks to the lochside, after tying a cast with a medium Butcher and a Peter Ross. Most of the rises were just out of reach. The weed was so heavy that it was difficult to find a space to cast in, and a big fish would certainly have been unplayable. Eventually I found some more sandy shallows. By wading out (in shorts) until the water was chest-deep, it was possible, in spite of the absence of ripple, to cast out to the nearest fish. The rod must have looked like a periscope, but no sooner had I landed the fly within range than it was taken with a bang.

In two of the most thrilling hours of my life I landed fifteen sea-trout and lost several more. If a seal had not come ashore after the shoal and scared them away out of reach it might have been a total of two dozen. Since then I have repeated the attempt and met with considerable success. But never, even at this spot, was I quite so lucky again.

In after years I migrated to Norfolk, where, at first from necessity and then from choice, I became a convert to the dry fly and the brown trout. All the same, dreams of the big silver fish and the tumbling waters keep returning. There is a sizeable movement of sea-trout down the east coast. Few rivers between Thames and Trent are fast or unpolluted enough to invite their patronage, but they nose round the estuaries in considerable numbers and come close inshore from June to August to roll in the shallows and rid themselves of sea-lice. Rumour has it that they are hardly ever caught on rod and line. Maybe. By way of reconnaissance, I went out with a netting party. Years ago, if I had been told that netting sea-trout could be a sport, I would have scoffed; but experience has forced me to admit that late-night sea-trout netting is most exciting. It can be uncomfortable and cold, but it is not necessarily so. Take a warm change of clothes, dry matches, plenty of food and a bottle of wine, choose your night carefully and all will be well.

A licence is not costly, but most of the fishing is done semi-professionally by local experts of long standing. They do not always welcome amateur help, but can be persuaded with luck. The nights when tide and weather are just right are few and far between, and opportunities are not lightly to be lost. The shores can be sand or shingle, and are quite deserted in the late evening. It is not advisable to start before dark.

The net is like a tennis net in shape, but longer. The bottom is weighted and there are cork floats along the top. One of the party, preferably the hardiest, wades waist-deep. The other stands at the edge of the water. When the net is 45° to 60° to the shore, both begin to walk parallel to the beach. The fish can be felt hitting the net and often seen as they try to make their escape from the 6in. deep rolling grounds. Sometimes they leap, and the sudden splash of silver is made even more dazzling by phosphorescent glitter. A thousand sparks speed away from one's feet at every step, and then shed stardust on breaking the surface. The beauty is exotically enchanting in a way that one could expect of the South Seas rather than that of grey old England. When it seems as if a number of fish are trapped in the angle of the net, the man at the deep end hurries inshore and both heave the catch. Anything may happen, but there will usually be a few great silvery trout; a blank is rare.

They run big in these parts. In most seasons trout of umpteen pounds are recorded, and one hears rumours of 20-pounders. Not the least fascinating part is the probability of finding strangers in the net, like crabs, mackerel (common or horse), dabs and turbot.

Back to a bonfire, to a change of clothes, a bottle of wine and a feast, and the glow of a happy return walk in the small hours.

On The Rocks

It is a hard life for the sea-trout fishing addict who finds himself being dried out by lack of means; austerity comes as a shock to the spoilt. Just before the war my father was able to take me up to one of the best rivers in the north—trout, sea-trout and salmon—with three miles of lovely water, a private sitting room, ample food and a nine-hole golf course for just £6 a week—an unbelievable sum today. Like many other enthusiasts, I find that my worldly success no longer enables me to give my sons a similar taste of heaven.

What then are the alternatives? A caravan makes two or three weeks in Scotland financially possible, but caravanning in the Highlands has changed out of all recognition. The splendid, lonely pioneering journeys of old have gone for ever. Not too long ago, to venture in a caravan through and beyond the old road through Glencoe was to leave civilisation. Passing places on the narrow roads with grass and heather flourishing down the middle were superfluous, because there never was other traffic to meet. One had the freedom of the whole north-west in which to park. Provided one was rain-proof, windproof and midgeproof, and able to prevent one's possessions from being eaten by Highland cattle, one could live out every man's dream in the bosom of nature.

The last time I went through Glencoe it was like Hyde Park on a Bank Holiday, with traffic nose to tail, and a piper with a curiously Lowland accent selling ice cream and tartan dolls. Anyone with a caravan attempting to camp by the roadside is ruthlessly tidied up and sent to the sites: rightly, for the verges would otherwise soon be disfigured by a mass of litter. The fishing propects for such caravanners are not too good. Hotels hire out some of their less good fishing to 'casuals'; lochs within easy walking distance are 'borrowed' with, or usually without, the agreement of the owners, but most good sea-trout fishing is just not available.

What has the law to say about fishing from the seashore in Scotland? I was brought up on the belief that the sea belongs to no man and the fruits thereof to all. The deep-sea fishermen may get involved in cod wars and there may be regulations limiting use of nets and night lines, but I have never discovered any limitations on the little-practised but noble art of fishing from the rocks with a small trout rod.

Oh, those rock pools of the sea-loch shores! There is nothing so beautiful in the length and breadth of Britain, nor so varied. In Harris, silver sand alternates with limpet-covered rocks and oar weed to make the sea a patchwork of emerald, jade and purple. One can wade out comfortably on gently shelving shell sand, or one can peer over cliffed promontories into the completely transparent depths of 30ft rock pools, where shrimps, cockles and anemones are shimmeringly clear.

In the farthest corners of Ardnamurchan, the little white beaches near Sanna and Ardtoe are still unspoilt. Their special magic is dominated by the mysterious silhouettes of Eigg, Muck and Rum and the jagged cool and distant Cuillins, suspended far away between the sea and skies in which sunsets glow and burn with ever-shifting flaring trails of transparent lava on an infinitely deep backcloth of turquoise. These sunsets are never the same, and each time one is convinced that there can never be another masterpiece like them.

If one never caught a fish, it would be heaven to spend one's days casting into the healing waters, listening to the oystercatchers, watching the patient herons, the buzzards and ravens wheeling in the evening light, or the cormorants wrestling with their catches. When the ripples die, there comes a mirror stillness on which a rising fish can be seen or heard a mile away.

But one does catch something: my son, serving his apprenticeship, caught lots. You can fish with almost anything; flies, wet or dry, sea-trout lures, mackerel feathers, spoons or spinners. And you never know what you will catch. Mackerel, of course, nearly always. How marvellously a big mackerel fights when he is hooked on an 8ft rod in among rocks and clumps of seaweed. Faster than a trout and just as beautiful. Then, every now and again, a different feeling as something heavier and slower bends the rod to a hoop: a pollack. Or the mad rush and thrill of a school of sea-trout moving its way along the coast towards fresh water. I once caught fifteen of them before breakfast.

If one should tire of the deep water, one can try the burn mouth or wade out into the flats, where the dabs and plaice, scudding and scurrying from under your feet, tempt you to resort to spearing; or, best of all, wade out at high tide into that unique short grass, striving to reach the mass of finnock playing and rising where the rocks start.

The fun is faster and more furious than all but the very best freshwater fishing. Of course, the skill and thrill of hooking and playing the fish in fast currents is lacking, but the unparalleled variety and beauty of the surroundings, together with the struggles with changing depths, treacherous seaweed and slippery rocks make it an apprenticeship second to none. And Scotland has, thank goodness, a length of coast equal to that of the rest of Europe, excluding Scandinavia, from the Baltic to the Black Sea.

April Fools in The Boat-House

Fishing is the one passion that grows increasingly feverish, uncontrollable and unreasonable with the passing years. As business preoccupations reduce present opportunities, and advancing age reduces future prospects, every moment spent rod in hand becomes more urgently precious.

Work, family and finance being organised, the Boat-house was booked for the first fortnight in April. I had not fished a loch in April for ten years, and adrenalin banished the exhaustion of a late night end-of-term conference. I got up at five o'clock for an all-day drive, collecting my family on the way, and when we exploded out of the overpacked car, the reward exceeded our dreams; a private loch, 400 yards by 300, and the prospect of a fortnight of unmitigated heaven.

Set in gentle hills, it had everything. A roe deer scampered away from the shore as we arrived. A heron was standing motionless in the reeds, and a buzzard soared overhead. The Boat-house was built out over the loch. There was ample room for four, it was comfortable and warm, the hot water was hot, and the lights worked. The view from the living-room took in the whole loch, so that the constantly changing pattern of reflections, ripples, rising trout and diving duck was visible from one's armchair and brought peace and beauty from dawn to dusk, and even afterwards. The hills were fresh and bright, with the Spring sun and clouds chasing across old bracken and new green.

We breathed deep, and the cares and troubles of heavy months dropped away as if by magic. It was too late to fish, so we calmed our fever as anglers do, by preparing for the morrow—testing the droppers, making vital decisions about the size and pattern of flies. Greenwell, of course. Butcher, or Tupp's Indispensable? Claret and Grouse, or Peter Ross or March Brown?

We were woken by the weird and romantic Spring song of the curlew. My unnatural eagerness led me to organise breakfast for the whole family, and to get them moving long before necessary. Although reason told me that nothing should be doing on April 1 before midday. I went down to the bank to get the feel of my rod again and to listen to the music of the reel. Within half an hour a splendid trout took me, fought like a demon and was safely netted at 1lb 10oz.

Back to the Boat-house and into the boat with my son. The lapwings were dashing down in their floppy display flights, and the whowing of their wings lifted my heart. The comforting creak of the rowlocks and the unfishy smell of fresh trout on my fingers brought back happy memories called from all over the Highlands. One forgets the chill, and the blisters, as one used to row into the teeth of gale-driven rain, and the hell of boredom and midges, and the miles of uphill trudging to unfruitful lochs.

Nothing happened for a drift of two, but we were not depressed. I was proud of my son's casting—no risk of time wasted on tangles here. Our lines shot out with perfect timing and gentle wrist work, hissing softly through the rings and landing all three flies softly, but in a straight line, even across the wind. An unwelcome cormorant had dropped in and in addition to the usual mallard and tufted duck, there were a pair of great-crested grebes and a dabchick.

'Don't take your eyes off the water, Bede; it's time for the beginning of the rise.' But the rise did not begin. Nor on April 2, 3, 4 or 5. We thrashed away from eleven until three every day. We comforted each other in traditional ways. 'They never rise in an east wind.' 'It's too early in the season for this part of the world, unless you get a warm spell. . . .'

We were glad to spend a couple of days visiting relatives, sight-seeing and replenishing stores and energy. On our return things did not improve much. Frost, then slush, and when the last day came we had only caught four or five more, and not as big as the first; there had been hardly any more seen rising. On the last morning we woke up to see the snow lying deep all round. The sky was thick with flurrying flakes, disappearing from a grim, dark sky into the dull lead mirror of the loch.

To prove our utter madness, we took the boat out into the blizzard and sat like Father Christmas and Captain Oates with the snow thick in our hair and lying on our shoulders, while our fingers froze to the bitterly cold line. From under our snow-bound eyebrows, to our utter astonishment we saw something like a rise. After the customary count of twenty-five to make sure it was not a dabchick or a tufted duck mocking our folly, we rowed over towards it. With visibility at barely fifty yards it was very hit and miss. There was a bold and boiling rise, and I struck it firmly; a lovely trout of just under 2lbs which ran and bored deep and fought marvellously.

Even a 20lb salmon could not have been more welcome. The longer you have suffered and struggled, the more glorious that moment of boil and pull, the more delicious the agony of playing and praying. We are, of course, mad; fortunately the fish are even more so. It is the one sport in which no rules are valid. April fools, all of us.

The Charm of Hill Lochs

What is the most attractive form of fishing? For all the rival claims of big-game fishermen, specimen-carp hunters, big barbel men or shore fishermen, there are two experiences which afford a pleasure sharper than any others: first, the swirl and surge as a heavy sea-trout or salmon snatches and bores deep and strong across the current making your line cut wings of water like a speed boat: second, the delicious suspense and delicacy of landing a dry fly lightly as a puss moth just above a substantial trout.

Sadly, both are becoming harder to find. Good sea-trout and salmon waters are expensive or over-crowded, and dry-fly rivers are little better. Waters too carefully tended become tame. Many of us fish to escape from civilisation and we are offended by neat stiles, scythed nettles or barbed wire blunted by sacking. The sameness of domesticated fish-farm trout, however large, stands in contrast to the variety of the lean hungry trout of the wilds, peat black, reed-bed yellow or pebbly speckled and red spotted.

If your special joy lies in the loneliness and beauty of nature, you can find it in the hill lochs, unspoiled, inexpensive and peaceful. From the age of eight, I have trudged through head-high bracken, groped my way with a landing net across quaking bog, scrambled up rock faces, manoeuvred my rod along burns overhung by trees, crossed peat, heather and myrtle to the realm of divers, buzzards and ravens, to the most beautiful places in the world—the hill lochs 3, 5, 10 or 15 miles from civilisation.

A long day's walk can encompass three or four entirely different lochs. You can start from an estuary with the smell of mussels and bladder-wrack in your nostrils, where the sunsets of turquoise and old gold will turn the sea to a blaze of glory and the silhouetted hills become stark and black. It is the haunt of seals and herons, cormorants and oystercatchers and great shoals of sea-trout and mackerel. You follow the river and the first tributary burn up through thick bracken and thinning birch woods, while the burn alternates white waterfalls and transparent rock pools framed in grey granite, green moss and scarlet rowan berries. It is hard work, but from the top there is a breathtaking view of the sea lochs and the distant ranges. Once over the top you are confronted with a rolling plateau over which the burn meanders slower and deeper through peat and marsh.

The first loch lies a mile from the burn over a low ridge. From the summit of that ridge you can glimpse a gleam of sea thirty miles away to the far north as well as the estuary left behind in the south, and if you are lucky, the enchanted, blue jagged outlines of the Cuillins, so distant they scarcely seem to be real.

This loch is rock-bottomed, half a mile long and 300 yards wide. The trout, fit and speckled, average nearly a pound; a few are much bigger. On the stormy days it is a funnel for the south-westerlies, and the wind howls and blusters, until the driving rain forces its way through your waterproof clothing, and sends you scuttling for shelter beneath the vast heather-covered boulders which surround its banks.

Two miles further on is a smaller, softer loch, like a figure of eight cuddled down between rocky banks, dry and heathery. Its clear water is a delight—sand, gravel, rock, and one small reed bed which harbours a pair of mallard. This second loch is nowhere more than four or five casts wide; the trout vary in size and colour, and there is always something doing. Fishing from the bank you are in a world of your own, unable to see more than a hundred yards in any direction; as sheltered as the first loch is exposed and cold.

From there you plod back upwards over the ridge to follow the burn to its source at the foot of a high mountain corrie. The source itself is little more than a marshy puddle, full of stunted, peaty, 4in. troutlet. Over the shoulder of the mountain, not far under 3000ft, is the loveliest of them all; a lochan in a kind of volcanic crater. Because it is so sheltered, its water is rarely more than fleetingly ruffled. Because it is invisible from the top and beyond the range of most ramblers and fishermen it is almost unknown. You are in eagle country and the great birds often soar across the high loch on their way to or from the crags on the far side of the mountain. A hundred yards farther on the views are stupendous; the lochside is, however, hidden. It is September, the stags are already belling and this is their favourite meeting place.

As evening draws on, the wind often drops and the silence is complete, except for the croaking of a raven or the call of a diver. The midges come out, and the still surface is broken by scores of tiny rings and dimples;

yellow trout up to half a pound in weight. They are hungry and naïve and rising in the clear sunlit water just as freely as they would in a steady ripple.

Now it is time to turn for home. It never gets quite dark, but to lose your way means a long, long walk. In the cool of the evening, little patches of mist rise like steam from the bottom of the valleys, and the lower lochs reflect first the glowing colours of the sunset and then the early stars. The smell of sun-drenched heather gives way to the freshness of bog myrtle and then of birch and bracken. When you reach the tree line you may be startled by the muffled stealthy flight of a barn owl. You may be lucky enough to glimpse a wild cat, for there are two or three families near the burn every year.

And so home to bed. In your mind's eye the lochs will file by, not just that night, but for ever . . . wooded and gentle, reedy and treacherous, rocky and savage, deep and shelving, shallow and sandy; small trout lochs, sea-trout lochs, ferox lochs to match every mood.

In Harris, in Appin, in Argyll, in Sutherland there are enough hill lochs to provide happiness for a thousand anglers prepared to walk 10 000 miles. Thank God, they may long survive oil and tourism, salmon disease and poaching. They will certainly survive you and me.

Call of The Waters

In the *Scots Magazine* there have been many wonderful descriptions and photographs of Scottish landscape. But what makes our scenery second to none is, above all things, water. It has been estimated that in sea coast alone, Scotland has as many miles as the rest of Europe from Leningrad round to the Black Sea. No one would even attempt to estimate the number of burns and inland lochs.

Not for me regrets about Scotland's high rainfall; even when, soaked and frozen, one drags oneself home through gales and sleet, or slops about with waders full after falling into a bog. Water and atmosphere are the poetry and essence of the Highlands.

Anglers and bird-watchers will agree that there is no mood or variety of flow, quality or setting that cannot be found between the Tweed and John O'Groats. When the exiled Scot closes his eyes to dream of home, he sees swirl and bubble and hears the gentle slapping of waves against the fat crude hull of some hill loch boat.

Each man's favourite water is a jewel that changes a hundred times according to mood and season, time, light and weather. Oh, that Schubert had been a Scot!

The musical gems inspired by a single mill stream would have been prolonged in an infinite profusion and variety.

How strong each memory comes back! One remembers, at the age of eight when all nature is twice as large as life and six times as exciting, leaning, greatly daring, over the edge of a small cliff plunging down into a Hebridean rockpool. Looking down from twenty feet into another fifteen feet of water, so clear that it seemed to magnify the cowrie shells on the bottom; so transparent that only the surge of weed and darting of fish gave it life.

Yet, past the narrow roaring neck of water, through which the pool emptied itself into the ocean, the transparency gave way to green, yellow and purple as the depth changed over successive layers of silver sand, anemone-covered rocks and giant oar-weed. Fish there were, of all shapes and sizes, crab and shrimps; and sometimes the glimpse of a whiskery lobster strayed from his cleft.

Different indeed to the miles of steep rocky shore with the slithery, burnt sienna wrack, which rides the tide for so many miles of the Argyllshire coast, with the smell of rotting iodine exasperating bathers and anglers alike. The bladder wrack nevertheless is a joy to the painter, and a paradise for heron and oystercatcher.

Every sea loch offers change. What more gloomy and frightening moods can water show than the chill, black fresh-water deeps of the Pass of Brander? What more smiling and cheerful than the sunlit panorama over the Forth from the Bass Rock to the Forth Bridge, seen from the highest point of the A68 before it dips down towards Edinburgh?

More intimate still to the angler are the differences between Tweed and Don and Spey. The big rivers are worlds in themselves which fill a fisherman's horizon. The Tweed is a hundred different rivers, grey or silver, red from the waters of the Leader, or green with floating weed in the summer drought that make fly fishing hell. But it is always recognisable for its dignity and power. In great August floods it swells in a matter of minutes to angry, dirty menace, sweeping along whisky bottles, mangold wurzels, sheep and picnic baskets.

The Spey is just a big fierce burn, beery in spate, frightening to wade in and full of Highland dash. It drives the gentler trout fishermen to seek refuge in its calmer and varied tributaries.

The Don is easier, smooth-banked and shingled, with big trout ready to rise as soon as the grey snow-water from the Cairngorms is clearing and the April sun brings a first comforting glow to the oilskin stretched over the angler's shoulders.

More personal are the hill lochs—lochs found by guesswork and prayer after miles of slogging through heather, bog, and bracken. Lochs in the alchemy of storm and sunshine, haunted by otters and loons, decimated by cormorants, protected by hordes of midges and soft clegs with green or orange eyes. Best of all, the loch which is each man's secret, still as remote and inaccessible as in his childhood, ringed in the calm of a West Highland sunset by dimpling fish, which alone break the silence deep as the Arctic night.

Of all Scottish waters, though, it is the burns that have most to say to the exile. Whether by the magic memory of the first trout fondled and treasured on their banks, or through the vision of waterfalls whose beauty has defied the skill of the great artists, their hold on us is unbroken.

From gurgling beginnings in the mountain bogs to the great pure rock pools cradled in fern and rowan, they are a delight as intimate, as rare and wild as any in the world. They have a unique power to wash away the wasted years, the mess, failure and muddle.

Heigh ho! It is holiday time, when the reel is taken out and given a nostalgic pull, and when the old fishing bag is inspected and its contents reviewed. The sound of the singing reel and the smell of the moorland and trout bring back the memory of the waters with so sharp a pang that all plans for the South of France can go to hell! It's back to the land of the dippers and buzzards for me.

Heaven, Hell and Purgatory

Tremble Tweed! Your master is at hand, and you are fated to be tamed again—by me, your conqueror in a hundred fights. The armoury is complete. The wet fly reel purrs like a nightjar; March Brown and Partridge and Orange are ready on a well tested 4lb breaking strain leader. There is a new rod, waders that are really waterproof, no holes in the net, and an oilskin to defy the worst that April can do. In the other flap of my fishing bag there is a dry fly reel, smooth as satin, with line well greased. On the bottom row of the fly box an array of Greenwell's blessed Glories, oiled, dry, hairy, upright and tempting.

Of course the weather could be better, with snow on the hills and more in the wind, but I haven't kept my nose to the desk all year to be deterred by such minor inconveniences. Thirty years of experience on the Tweed tells me that the first flies will be taken by trout between 12.30 and 1.00 pm.

So into the car and down the hill to a spot 200 feet above the river. The Tweed here is at the bottom of a lovely, deep valley: Scott's view which adorns a thousand table mats. A steep and slippery path leads down the wooded bank to a thunderously splendid salmon pool. A couple of goosanders fly up the river, grey wagtails are flashing on the shingle and a dipper is bobbing away in the shallows. Odds fish! But how I love that place! As I peer down at the pool a salmon jumps, and my heart with it. But it is the trout I'm after. In spite of the bitter north wind and the first snowflakes stinging my face even in the shelter of the woods and of the deep valley, the unbearable excitement of a new season is so hot within me that I forget the caution and dignity proper to my years and break into a run. With the momentum of two hundred-weight and inadequately studded waders the trot becomes an accelerating and uncontrollable hurtle and, finally, an ignominious skid and fall ends in a torn oilskin jacket and a backside covered with mud.

Bruised and a little sobered, but still childishly and feverishly eager, I waddle onto the shingle. As I put my tackle together, the music of the waters fills me with wild joy. The river is clear and a little low; there are no flies on the water. Not quite midday; it would be unreasonable to expect trout to rise in such weather before one o'clock. I'll try wet fly in the broken water above the pool.

By this time the wind is achieving the impossible by blowing straight from the opposite bank—out of the face, so it seems, of the sheer 200 foot hill which rises direct from the water's edge. For some extraordinary reason the line won't sink. Some ass must have greased it, or handled it with greasy fingers. Perhaps it was me? Even with some lead shot nipped on, the wretched thing floats as if bewitched. I thrash the water in vain for two hours, while wind and snow grow fiercer and more stinging. By two o'clock I feel like Captain Oates making his supreme sacrifice. The snow is now driving parallel to the water, not falling into it, and my eyelashes are developing icicles. As I turn towards the shore to seek shelter and eat sandwiches, my waders slip on the slimy, weedy slope of one of those treacherous traps, half boulder, half shelving rock, in which the Tweed specialises. I reel, stagger and plunge; a kind of dance of death from which I shall recover, at the expense of a wrenched back and a torn hamstring; in the meantime I drop my net into four feet of water. I recover it before it is swept out of my depth, by getting my left arm soaked to the shoulder and my sandwiches soggy beyond edibility. Trudging back upstream along the cliff's foot is a hard task at the best of times; in a blizzard, with a damaged leg, it is indescribable. Throwing a fly into one or two of the favourite haunts leads to another slip and the other wader full of icy water.

The only fish seen is a large diseased salmon which is blind enough to let me nearly tread on it, but powerful enough to give me a hell of a fright, as it bolts for the deep water right between my legs.

A tiny slackening in wind and snow persuades me to stay on to try a dry fly, even though nothing is rising, and no fisherman in his senses would persist in such weather. For some incalculable reason, as I turn for the last time for the land a large trout seizes the fly. I am not paying attention, and the reel handle catches in the hole in my oilskin, so that the leader breaks: an incident which persuades me to stay for another hour to the verge of pneumonia, with only one 7oz trout, whose brains must presumably have given way under the piercing cold, to show for my pains.

What a day! Inefficient, unprofitable, painful, danger-ous, miserable. It is just a crazy paradox that this senseless, useless, protracted suffering should be crowned by a glow of happiness brought on by a hot bath and a stiff gin and an exhausted evening stupor of well-being beyond the contrivance of the greatest gourmets and sensualists. Are Scottish fishermen just masochists? Or does intensity of pleasure depend on the sharpness of precedent pain?

By the next day, Saturday the 12th, the snow has stopped and melted, and I arrive, repaired and restored, at the great salmon pool, punctually at 11.30 am. The sun has broken through, heating the oilskin over my shoulders, and chaffinches and blackbirds are singing. All the pain of yesterday is soothed away. The snow water is already clearing and a few brave flies are sailing down the river. At the bottom of the pool one or two fish start to mop them up . . . the eddy where they are waiting is, inevitably, in a slightly awkward place beyond the fastest part of the stream, which makes it almost impossible to avoid a drag on the fly. Nevertheless, my third cast brings me a splendid rise and although there is a big sag in my line and my strike is late, I land a trout of 1¼lbs, in splendid condition. A few casts later I get another good trout, and then a more sluggish fighter which turns out to be a grayling.

By then I have put down that small group, but the hatch is coming down in ever greater numbers. I hurry up past the long pool where very few trout are taking. At the tail of the next salmon pool two wet fly fishermen are casting, in desultory fashion, at half a dozen trout which are taking steadily in smooth though powerfully moving water slightly ruffled by the breeze. We exchange a few words, and they reel in and climb out, inviting me to have a shot, as the trout seem quite uninterested in their wet flies. In two minutes I have three more trout of over a pound—splendid fighters in the strong stream at the tail of the pool, nearly thwarting my efforts to keep them out of the roaring, tumbling rapids which would have swept them beyond the control of my little 8ft rod. It is like a dream; the fly lands just right, the fish take boldly, and everything that rises is landed. I put back several under ¾lb. Before the rise finishes I have kept nine weighing 8½lbs.

Hell and Heaven on successive days! Pure joy, in which the discomfort of my brother fishermen plays its part, and the eyebrow lifting of the locals who refuse to believe in dry fly gives me vicious delight. Not the gentle art, my tumultuous and conceited emotions are a blend of Toad at the Wheel and Muhammed Ali after victory.

On Tuesday the 15th however, the Tweed has something different in store. An ideal day, warmer, with the water rising but, to begin with, unduly coloured. Plenty of fly. By one o'clock the trout are rising furiously to a hatch like a regatta. Most ignore me. I rise two or three and lose them all. I waste precious minutes changing leader and fly, wondering whether a small knot in the nylon and a slightly blunt hook might be responsible for my failure. The rise grows to a crescendo as squadrons, flotillas and fleets of what seem to be the same fly as Saturday are gulped by large trout on all sides. Nothing looks at me and the rise slackens with only one half-pounder to show for nearly two hours of feverish fishing. Turning my attention to the rougher water I promptly rise and hook a substantial sea-trout. My reel screams and my rod bends like a croquet hook. Suddenly the fly comes back, for no apparent reason.

In blundering after the sea-trout I had gone as far down the comparatively shallow rocks in the middle of the river as possible. I realised that the water had been rising, thanks to some storm in the hills; quite suddenly it had become not merely beery but muddy, opaque and hostile, hurling down its usual mixture of whisky bottles, motor tyres, tennis balls and branches. Trying to stagger back against the current over treacherous channels which could no longer be identified I lost my footing and landed flat on my back with only my rod rising like a periscope above the water.

When mother and daughter welcomed me back and asked me if I had had a good day, I was not sure how to answer. The Tweed had definitely won and had the last word. To fish it is like living a Greek tragedy . . . nemesis follows inevitably on the heels of hybris. Like life itself it is six to four against; the fleeting joys must be paid for by sorrows. Whether it smiles or frowns it takes complete possession and drains everything else away. Therein lies its great and healing strength.

Of Burns and Worms

When anyone complains that the Western Highlands in places average over 100 inches of rain a year, I feel nothing but thankfulness; for the soul of Scotland is, above all, visible in its waters. The rich charm of the hill lochs, the dark grandeur of the Awe, the prosperous majesty of Don and Dee, the rocky tumbling of the Spey, the magic of the distant Cuillins suspended between the setting sun and the glowing sea: each is an individual world with its own devotees. But the burns are every man's; in their inexhaustible variety they are the refuges to which true country Scots ultimately return.

Most of us served our apprenticeship on local burns. While fathers and elder brothers rowed up and down the loch, or fished the tidal pool for sea-trout in orthodox and undemanding comfort, it was understandable that they should wish for a holiday from disentangling irretrievably-knotted casts for eight-year-olds. So the youngest were banished to humbler waters, perhaps only dimly aware of how privileged they were.

I had an 8ft, black metal rod, wisely chosen for me because it was strong enough to stand up to being trodden on or poked into rock faces while clambering along river banks. It was also infinitely manoeuvrable. Off I went, in shorts and gym shoes; into my little fishing bag, still smelling of trout, were crammed tomato and sardine sandwiches, cheese and biscuits, an orange and a bottle of ginger-beer, in uneasy proximity to a tin of worms kept fresh with earth and moss.

Eight hours a day of absolute freedom, no grown-ups to fuss, to advise or to forbid. I learnt by trial and error, with an occasional hint from a tactful father. Single-hook worm-casts are not so prone to tangles and breakages as three-fly loch casts; but let no-one assume that their use demands less skill.

On what grounds do we presume to believe that our graduation from worm to wet fly, from wet fly to dry fly or dapping, and from dry fly to spinning for salmon is in any sense real progress? True , the worm is messy; to impale a living creature, however insensitive, is unattractive. Admittedly a worm-baited hook is more likely to damage a fish than is an artificial fly. Undoubtedly worm-fishing can, under some condi-tions, be too efficient; I saw a small boy who had caught thirty sizeable trout in one pool on an 'exclusive' river on which I had been a guest for a day.

Perhaps worming is not so delicately satisfying an art as that of casting perfectly with a dry fly, nor does it always attract such large fish as the cumbersome winding of ironmongery does. But skill it certainly requires, and I suspect that the main reason why the middle-aged abandon the worm is that they find it increasingly difficult to submit their corpulent figures to the contortions necessary for successful stalking.

In spate conditions it can be an easy game. Every crofter's son knew where the takeable trout lay in the swirling backwaters of the slower pools in the lower part of the glen. My greatest joy, however, was to go up into the hills on a fine day and to try my hand at clear-water worming. Once I was 500ft above the glen I never saw another human being.

Where the burn came tumbling down the steep slopes, I could stand in the water with my head barely level with the surface of the next pool upstream. It was possible to fish the lovely deep pools at the foot of the waterfalls quite unseen. Is water so clear anywhere else in the world?

The rocky banks were overhung by rowans heavy with a riot of scarlet berries, and the moss-clad boulders behind the falls offered nesting sites for the dippers and grey wagtails that were my constant companions. When the sheltered ravine grew too hot, it provided marvellous bathing.

Over the brow of the hill, the burn slowed and became deeper and more 'peaty' in colour. Before it started to meander across the plateau it ran over a pebbly stretch flanked by patches of brilliant gorse. There you could eat your lunch while the sun heated the mackintosh across your shoulders, then lie intoxicated by the heady smell of blossom. Yellow hammers, bright as the bloom itself, and stonechats, red, white and black, ticked away from the top of every clump.

The plateau was the haunt of grouse, curlew and buzzards. The burn here held bigger fish—not over half-a-pound, but they seemed giants to me and fought like demons. The banks became abrupt and treeless as the burn cut its way through peat, and you had to stalk Indian-wise, crawling on your stomach. I could see neither the fish, the water, nor even the greater part of the line; the moment for the strike had to be judged by spotting a momentary check in the line's progress downstream as it left the rod point. The fishing could be exciting.

Every burn demands differences in fishing technique. Not all hold only small fish, and I have had my breathtaking adventures with salmon and sea-trout. How much does the size of a burn, as opposed to the acidity of the water, the temperature, the soil and the feeding, govern the size of the trout? I remember being astonished to see a Frenchman catch a 2lb trout in a tiny ditch not 2ft across near the Plateau de Langres. The stream plunged into a tunnel beneath a tangle of undergrowth.

The Frenchman—using a spinning reel—released his worm at the upstream-end and floated it down for twenty yards before it was taken. Avoiding snagging the undergrowth seemed more a case of luck than judgment. With strong nylon and utter ruthlessness he wound the fish straight back up the tunnel, later assuring me that he had caught many other trout in the same way. I believe the nature of the banks and the available food are the decisive factors governing the size of the burn trout.

Bigger streams yield good results to worm cast upstream and across on a long line. The worm is allowed to roll down a pebble-covered bed. The method is so successful on the Tweed that it should perhaps be controlled.

In general, burn-fishermen used to avoid using floats, but the development of the bubble-float has meant that downstream fishing with worms can be tremendously rewarding. A few years ago I watched the chef at a Highland hotel fishing. His sole object was to catch as many sea-trout for dinner as quickly as he could, and he got eight good sea-trout in an hour by unerring, long-casting and by float-fishing worms along the edge of a deep pool where overhanging trees prevented flyfishing.

A limit should be set on catches made on worm, not because worm-fishing is unskilled or unsporting, but in order to preserve stocks.

While motoring in Invernesshire not long ago I saw from a name on a map that I had stumbled on a burn much fished by my father and uncle as children. There was just time before sunset to find an attractive pool so surrounded by rowans that from only one place could you swing a worm with the utmost caution into the stream.

I brought it off, and a really big fish got hold—a sea-trout, I think. The rod bent, the reel screamed—and the nylon parted, snagged on an overhanging branch. All the happy days on the burns came flooding back to mind. I shall take my sons back again before it is too late.

Seals, Sea-Trout and Bladder Wrack

Among the scores of lovely and varied sea lochs in Scotland, there is one which embraces nearly all their qualities. A little river flows into its landlocked end where the glen is perhaps five hundred yards wide. It meanders through half a square mile of that unique West Highland seaside grass, so short that it looks as though it were mown daily, so pale bleached by the high tides that it is more silver than green. The grass gives way to boulders covered with iodine coloured bladder wrack. At low tide an old sea-trout trap, long disused, becomes visible. It once consisted of a dam of boulders about four feet high with a small gap in the middle. At high tide the shoals of trout and salmon would come up into the tidal pool; as the tide ebbed the local fisherman would walk out along the top of the dam and net the fish trying to escape back into the loch. The little boulder dam has now collapsed; but it is still a convenient though dangerous way of wading out to reach the deeper water. It is also encrusted with excellent mussels. At high tide it is entirely hidden except for the wrack which lifts and drops with the movements of waves and tide.

On each side of the loch there is a narrow strip of rocky coast interspersed with a few sandy or muddy flats beside the pebbly beds of the burns. There is room for a narrow and winding road ten feet above high tide, and beyond the road the steep slopes of the hills are covered with birch and rowan to a height of 500 feet. This loch and mountain scenery is transfigured by the continually shifting light, and especially by the most enchanting sunsets, and the estuary is so full of fish that every kind of bird and animal comes down to share the spoils: herons at all times, at low tide the oystercatchers and sandpipers and, as the tide comes in, the seals and the cormorants following the shoals of sea-trout and mackerel. Every evening a dozen ravens and an equal number of buzzards gather over the estuary and give a marvellous display of soaring against the spectacularly changing turquoise, purple, old gold and vermilion of the sky and the loch.

Nowadays would-be campers are swept up into the new site, placed quite rightly, for the sake of tidiness, a few miles up the loch. In the days before the mass invasion of the Western Highlands it was possible to camp on the short grass above high tide, and to be alone. The postmistress at the nearest tiny village still spoke Gaelic, as did most of her customers.

The most delightful feature of that marvellous place was the sea fishing. When high tides coincided with dusk or dawn the fun was especially fast and furious. To save time, I would go to bed in shorts, with my rod and landing net leaning at the ready against the caravan, complete with sea-trout flies: butcher, mallard and silver. My impatience would wake me up before dawn, to the exasperation of my long-suffering family. I would draw aside the curtains and peer hopefully at the water only twenty yards away. First the commotion of a solitary seal heading and tailing its way up the shallow waters like a great grey salmon. I would then rush from the caravan pulling on a sweater and grabbing the rod and net as I ran. The seal would withdraw, and I would watch for the dimples of the quietly rising sea-trout in the gaps between the seaweed. Very quickly, I would feel my way into the salt water. Wading was not easy, and there was little ripple at dawn. The rocks were large and the weed slippery, though the clusters of mussels gave some unreliable purchase to gym shoes. Invariably the sea-trout were rising at the extreme limit of my reach. In the still water any splash was fatal, and the stalking of the shoal required an almost Indian stealth. A false step would plunge one into deep water and frighten the fish irretrievably. If one hooked a respectable sea-trout close to the shore the chances of losing it in the seaweed were very high. So I would venture out until the chill waters rose over my shorts and half way up my chest. To cast the longest possible line, I had to wave my 8 ft rod uncomfortably above my head, almost like a periscope. In the end I would reach the nearest of the shoal, and if I could avoid a splashy cast, they rose unfailingly. Striking was difficult; a very long line does not help quick response, and there was seldom any wind to straighten it or current to pull it straight. If one's face is a bare 18 inches above water it is not easy to see the rise or to manoeuvre a fish over one's net. Balanced on slippery rocks, steering fish clear of seaweed with light tackle and a frail rod, the odds were barely even.

One such morning I caught fifteen before breakfast. Even if the sea-trout were not on the boil, there was always fun with the mackerel whose first rush is almost as swift as a ¾lb finnock. Occasionally there would be surprises: the slow and heavy pull of a substantial pollock, or of a large soft-mouthed white fish.

Within an hour and a half the sea-trout would be gone out of reach, and I would clamber back, realising for the first time that I was blue with cold. A quick change and a warm-up, grilling sea-trout and mackerel for the family, was followed by a trip to the local farmer to offer him a share of our spoils in exchange for his latest gossip about the otters, wild cats, and eagles which were his neighbours.

Life was not always so smooth. The sea breezes were not always sufficient to save us from the merciless attention of the Highland midges, and we took to a caravan because our tent was eaten by Highland cattle. On another occasion my attempt to rescue one of the farmer's sheep which had become marooned on a tiny island by the swiftly incoming tide was crowned with humiliation. The terrified animal was 100 yards from dry land and bleating its heart out. I stripped and swam out to it, only to see it step happily into the water and swim a great deal better than I.

But it is in learning such simple country truths that the real enjoyment lies. For the time being the Scottish shore belongs to no man and the fruits thereof to all.

Putting a Fly Over The Germans and The French

Many British anglers assume that if they want to catch fish anywhere else in Europe they must look either to Scandinavia or Austria. There can, indeed, be little to rival these countries for variety and size of trout. But for those who want good value less far afield in a warmer and drier climate, Germany and France also have much to offer.

Germans provide excellent information about the nature of their fishing, where to apply for permits and so on. The traditional fisherman's licence to exaggerate quantity and size seems not to have taken hold of the Teutons as much as it has elsewhere. The German Tourist Information Bureau provides an exhaustive and detailed report some 30 pages long, arranged by districts, and telling one where to apply and how much the different types of permit cost. Wisely, it does not commit itself deeply as to the relative quality of rivers or districts. Protection of private beats can be fairly fierce, but many excellent waters are cheap compared with British standards, provided one is not afraid of filling up forms.

After contacting the G.T.I.B. the wise traveller will arm himself with Varta, a hotel guidebook which, though less well known here than the Michelin, can bear comparison with it. A charming feature of Varta is its use of nightcaps as a symbol for hotels away from the rush and the roar of the traffic. If the nightcap is red, the surroundings are beautiful and quiet. Rocking-chairs and wrought-iron signs are further eloquent symbols which help build up a most vivid picture.

Another advantage is that it goes lower down the financial scale, so that the angler of slender means can easily find his home from home. German hotels are clean and their prices are low; the more beautiful and isolated the part of the country, the lower the prices. Food is not exciting, especially if one does not like wurst. But, once one is used to the technique of dealing with the federbett in country districts, the inns are comfortable and pleasant.

The art of coping with this amorphous mass of feathers always eludes some people. If it is placed longitudinally, the draught finds a way in, one side or the other: if it is placed latitudinally, one's toes stick out and freeze. Get it just right on a hot night and one suffocates or boils. But those who have served their apprenticeships find it the best form of all bed-clothing.

The main fishing areas, though by no means the only ones, are the Eifel, the Sauerland, the Lahn and its tributaries, the Black Forest and the foothills of the Alps in Bavaria and Baden-Wurttemburg. In the smaller streams the trout are numerous and often surprisingly large. The rivers sometimes bear grayling too. The dry-fly fisherman is a rare bird, and the fish are unsophisticated in their approach to his wares. Some years ago the Ahr was surprisingly good. It had

beautiful scenery and an abundance of trout and
grayling, as well as one of the rare German red wines.
But there are signs that pollution and too much tourism
have wrought serious damage and permission to fish is
difficult.

Bavaria offers the most varied waters for exploration.
How many tourists have licked their lips to see fat trout
swimming nonchalantly in the stream running through
the streets of Oberammergau within a landing-net's
sweep of the pavements which form its banks! There are
large lake trout, hard to catch except with hardware,
little trout in the rushing streams and bigger ones lower
down the valley, and friendliness and hospitality often
more striking than anywhere in Germany. Nearly
twenty years ago my wife and I stayed in a Bavarian inn
in a room with a balcony and bathroom overlooking a
lake and a crocus meadow with a view of the Alps and
deer playing by the lakeside every evening. The inn had
a television room, a good bar with charming clientele,
and charged twenty-five shillings for bed and breakfast
for both of us!

In France, the sun-seeking angler has more certainty
of warmth. Food will be better, but more costly, the
price of hotels much more varied, and information less
objective. The French fishing community has the same
charm and some of the same unreliability as the Irish.
The descriptions are glowing, but where and whenever
one goes fishing the fish were always at their best last
week, or will be next month, or they never rise when the
temperature is above or below 25°C. or . . .

Nevertheless, there are beautiful fish to be caught,
from the splendid grayling of the Doubs to the trout
streams of Brittany; fat trout even below the Pont du
Gard and on countless rivers and lakes of the foothills of

the Pyrenees, the Alps, the Cevennes, the Jura, the Ardennes, the Massif Central, the tributaries of Dordogne, Lot and Tarn and the huge, strange trout of the Vosges lakes, supposed to be landlocked salmon. If one knows where to look, there are trout of more than 5lb to be caught in several of these places, even in the main stream of the Dordogne. The fact that the locals use maggots, grasshoppers, bacon rind or bunches of hen feathers, does not preclude the success of Greenwell's Glory.

The great charm of French fishing is that the enthusiasts are so proud of their water that they are delighted to share their joy. It is only human if the best is sometimes a closely guarded secret. And the bureaucracy of French fishermen is delightfully human and helpful. Where else would one write to a complete stranger on one of the Southern departments, masquerading under the title of the president of the Federation of the official societies of Fishing and Pisciculture, and receive as charming a reply as this?

Dear Sir,
Thank you for your letter of the 22nd, I enclose a summary of the fishing opportunities in our department. As you intend to stay near N and to fish dry fly, I could strongly recommend the Hotel C on the River V. Pension terms are very cheap, and I hope that you will use my name as a recommendation there and at Mr. D's shop nearby, who will supply any of the necessary equipment. Mr. D. would also be delighted to show you the best spots for fly-fishermen. The pub is close to the intersection of two first-class trout rivers and there is another excellent tributary.
If you are able to get to S. I would be delighted to offer you a drink and to give you any more detailed tips straight from

the horse's mouth.

signed
(The President of the Federation)

Where else could it happen? Who could resist the invitation?

But one warning; avoid August.

Casting Moss Before Carp

I needed a trip to the Rhône Valley to make me realise that *pêche à la mousse* is neither gastronomic French for frothed up peaches and cream nor a lisper's description of fly fishing. Although it is an ancient custom and one that is practised locally in England (for roach, for instance, from Norfolk weirs) it owes its present status in France to the beaked carp.

For some reason the beaked carp has never caught on in England. The British have never shared the German passion for carp, and this supposed relative is no great loss to our tables. It has muddy flesh and a long nose, its characteristic expression is haughty and mournful.

For the fishermen of eastern France, however, and especially for those from the Rhône and its tributaries, interest in the beaked carp has become a necessity. Since its introduction from Germany in the nineteenth century the 'hotu', as it is called, has taken over so thoroughly that it is in danger of swamping other fish by sheer weight of numbers. Look over any bridge on the Ognon, and you will see them packed shoulder to shoulder, between half a pound and a pound or a little more, their sides flashing in the August sun as they lazily flip over to mop up any food the river is washing down to them.

By the standards of fishermen who would otherwise be mainly concerned to catch as many ablettes (bleak) and goujons (gudgeon) as possible for a friture, this is big game. The hotu gives a surprisingly good fight—not unlike its neighbour, the grayling, which does so well in Saône tributaries like the Doubs. It is even more difficult than the grayling to catch by the orthodox methods. Paste, maggots or flies get very meagre results considering the dense shoals of fish, and I have found it easier to catch them by foul hooking with a wet fly than by worming. Much the greatest success, however, is achieved by *pêche à la mousse*; in the right places no other method seems to be contemplated by the locals.

The method is this; you stand on the forward slope of a weir, dam or waterfall, where there is a generous growth of moss over shallow rock and stone, take a small hook lightly weighted with shot, drag it through the moss until a three-quarter-inch tail of green slime has accumulated, and then you swim it down the eddies at the side of the head current of the deep pool below you. Not only does this method catch great numbers of beaked carp, but quite a few roach and bleak, and even an occasional grayling and perch. I saw one moss fisherman hook a pike, although one should not admittedly deduce too much from that, as there is scarcely a bait that has not at some time claimed such a success. Using 16ft cane rods with very flexible tips, no reels and fine nylon, a lot of ground is covered, and a long landing net and much skill are needed to land the bigger fish.

Some of the experienced *pêcheurs à la mousse* believe that the hotus are not truly vegetarian, but eat the moss for the sake of the quantity of little insects which are to be found in it as small fragments are washed downstream by the waterfalls. Be that as it may, specimens I examined were so full of moss that green slime was oozing from their vents. The hotu is reported to be quite good to eat, but I found this reputation hard to understand. French sauces and methods of preparation are so elaborate that they can make pike and roach into prized dishes. As long as the original flavour is hidden, all is well.

I make no plea for introducing the beaked carp into England, but coarse fishermen with a taste for travel and novelty should seek it out in its home waters, like the Ognon at Marnay—no tourists, nice people, beautiful quiet scenery, kingfishers, little bitterns, and harriers. Licences are moderately priced and if you feel the need for more variety and excitement, it is only a short drive to the trout streams of the Jura or the splendid grayling of the Doubs. The height of the moss season falls in August, when other forms of fishing are not at their best. Last and not least, it is perhaps the cheapest way of fishing.

By Streams

Overpopulation and overpopularity are in danger of making trout-fishing in England a rich man's sport. Only the remoter parts of Ireland and Scotland still provide good cheap fishing, and it needs more and more determined seeking and walking to avoid private beats or caravan-infested public waters. Within 200 miles of London, every promising piece of river which holds trout is bristling with bailiffs, freed of all obstacles, lavishly provided with stiles and available to selected members of the establishment at exorbitant prices. The presence of any lie with sizeable fish is betrayed by a trampled bank and the well-worn groove of countless kneeling pads.

Recently, I took a holiday in Germany, and a friend offered to take me on a fishing trip. To my astonishment, the stream to which I was led was only 3ft wide and 18in. deep (except for a few holes of perhaps 2½ft) with a sandy bottom, making it gin-clear. As the banks consisted of tangled undergrowth more than head high, I suspected a practical joke or a mistake and nearly gave up even attempting to fish. I did, however, walk a little way upstream. Where the stream ran through a wood, the bottom changed colour a little, and one or two fish were dimpling in the shadows. Under difficult conditions, I managed to drop a fly within range. The majesty of the resultant swirl and the size of the trout caught were a revelation.

This set me thinking. Brought up fishing wet fly on Highland rivers and lochs, I had not realised, even through burn worming experience, what tiny streams can contain respectable trout. Ever since, I have kept my eyes open for small tributaries overlooked by even the most optimistic fisherman. I found plenty of others in Germany, and it has since become apparent that it is not a peculiarity of Teutonic trout. To my surprise, it turned out that there are many such streams, even south of the Wash. The farmers owning the banks are fortunately unaware that they own good trout water. The tangled undergrowth by the stream-side and the small size of the stream itself makes them believe that the fish are uncatchable, or that it is not worth the expense of clearing the banks and paying a bailiff. So the trout, in untroubled isolation, wax fat and confident.

To some, such fishing can appear trying, and indeed it is no game for beginners. To begin with, one must be prepared to force one's way through hedges, barbed wire, blackberries, nettles, marsh, mud and undergrowth; to endure horse-flies, wasps' nests and midges, and to fish under conditions of acute discomfort and difficulty. That, however, is the source of the most perverse and secret delights of trout fishing. Your wealthy fisherman who gets his bag of good artificially reared and pampered trout from rivers with sleek, well-kept banks, does not taste the same triumphs. He does not know the satisfaction of getting large numbers of trout from water where no-one else is prepared to fish, or where others lose so many flies and casts that they remove their custom, finding it cheaper to pay large rents, avoid tangles and save their equipment.

The greatest essentials of by-stream dry-fly technique are:—

1. A short rod, preferably 7ft 6in.
2. Infinite stealth and patience.
3. An ability to manoeuvre one's fly both on the back and on the forward cast and in cramped conditions to within two or three inches.
4. The finest gut or nylon.

When a stream is completely enclosed by trees or undergrowth, wading is inevitable and it is important to realise that a real artist can reach a stance (or crouch) within half-a-dozen feet of a trout in crystal-clear water, provided that he doubles himself up so that his head is no more than two feet above water-level and that his rod is not allowed to flash over the place where the trout is lying. Most difficult and most important of all, no waves or vibrations must disturb the fish. Where there is little or no current or wind and the surface is glass smooth, this requires heron-like quietness of movement. A quarter of an hour may have to be devoted to stalking a selected trout from a distance of ten yards. If you are not prepared to do this, you will never succeed, and you would do well to hire a beat on the Test, or go and fish for salmon with a barge-pole.

The choice of clothing and equipment is also important. On a Summer's day in the South of England, heavy waders are not only clumsy but exhausting during the approach marches. Anyone who has waded in two feet of mud will remember the frightening and laborious process of extracting one leaden leg after the other, like a giant wasp in a sea of molasses. Shorts and plimsolls are suicidal unless one is nettle-proof. The only satisfactory answer appears to be an old pair of long corduroys, tough enough to withstand brambles and nettles and warming to the backside even when wet. This is not a game for the old and stiff or those susceptible to colds, as it may require complete stillness for long periods in three feet of water, following overheated struggles through the English jungle. And let no one underestimate the English jungle. Brazilian explorers used to hacking their way forward inch by inch in the torrid heat might well be surprised by what the home counties can offer in size of thorn and toughness of creeper.

In my particular area of England, there are four or five such jungle streams within a dozen miles. In some cases, their lower reaches are known to the general fishing public and are privately owned. It is my experience, however, that the fish are no smaller in these upper reaches though they might well be banished were the banks to be cleared, bailiffs installed and stocking and dredging carried out.

This year, armed with farmers' permission, I have been out many times to these waters. Only twice have I failed to bring back more than four trout. Though their size is not great, they have averaged something over ½lb, with the occasional pounder. The fight afforded on a 7ft 6in. rod in confined quarters and amongst weeds with 2lbs breaking strain nylon is out of all proportion to the actual weight of the fish. Not only does the continual struggle against the resistance of nature afford the maximum of frustration and of triumph, but the Indian stealth demanded brings one to see a wealth of wild life that remains hidden even to the ordinary fisherman: intimate glimpses of kingfisher, vole, heron, coypu—and at times an otter.

For a man still fit and young it offers fun comparable

with the best that the famous chalk streams of the south can offer.

Vive Greenwell!

Faith makes the great fishing fly. The very ring of their names proclaims the maker's confidence: Greenwell's Glory, Wickham's Fancy, Tupp's Indispensable. Each true angler has a favourite, of his own tying or of a little known pattern, which brings him success when all else fails: for my father it was a Mallard and Silver for sea trout; for brown trout an ancient and hairy horror like a March Brown with an Afro-Asian hairstyle, which proved incredibly endurable and chalked up a few score large victims in all manner of unsuitable conditions.

My choice, however, is commonplace. A dry Greenwell is the king of flies. It would be vain to list the successes it has brought me over the years; the experience is, I am sure, shared by a majority of fishermen. In lazy middle age, while others more energetic and knowledgeable are wasting the fleeting afternoon rise searching through their immaculate fly boxes for perfect matching patterns, I thrash on with Greenwell, and reap devotion's reward. Admittedly my faith goes to excessive lengths. Since the day I hooked three large sea-trout in one pool on the Tweed on my smallest size of dry Greenwell, I have over-used it at home and abroad, in muddy lakes and clear torrents, in fresh water and salt.

Like many married trout fishermen, my greatest problem is that my wife likes the sun. Once she was left in a caravan in Ardnamurchan to face three weeks of almost unbroken rain. Never was there such killing of sea-trout, but it is understandable that to play snakes and ladders and ludo all day, with bored children of three and seven, in the hopes that any interval in the rain will not bring intolerable torture from midges, is not everyone's idea of fun. Since then my Scottish holidays have been strictly rationed, and I have had to serve a substantial sentence in the South of France.

The 'Midi' has many merits. If the trout fishing were first-class, there would be no complaints. Somewhere below that magic line through the 'Massif central' below which the brussels sprout is unknown and the apple flourishes not, there are places where the heat of the sun is not such as to make all respectable trout give up the ghost. There are miles of wild and beautiful rivers supposedly bearing quantities of large trout, and the fishing is cheap and available. Unfortunately my holidays are limited to August and trout fishing in the 'Midi' is at its best early in the year. At the opening of the season, the French descend on their rivers with grass-hoppers, nymphs, maggots, centipedes, giant caterpillars, spinners, spears, nets and grenades. Most surviving trout die of heat or take refuge in such remote mountain streams as to daunt their most relentless pursuers. To plan a family holiday round such haunts is a major problem.

On this visit the temperature just north of Carcassonne was 40° Centigrade at the end of July and beginning of August. The river Orbie offered a chance of fishing, or at least of escape from heat stroke. It is a lovely fast-flowing river winding its way through rocky gorges, with little villages perched on the hillsides every five or six miles. The bathing was marvellous, although the water was too warm to offer hope of trout at that time of the year. Nevertheless there were masses of fish in the pools, some of considerable size. One never quite knows in the south what these fish will turn out to be: sun perch, beaked carp or barbel?

The locals were turning up stones on the bank and fishing (without much success) with the oversized creepy-crawlies that emerged. A few larger fish were rising under the trees at the edge of the biggest pool.

When I swam across the pool clad in bathing trunks and a floppy hat designed to avert sunstroke, holding a trout rod aloft in one hand to keep the line dry, the locals shrugged their shoulders. When I swam back to repeat the process for my landing net, they laughed outright. But they must have been even more incredulous when they saw the 'mad Englishman' wading up to his neck and wielding his little rod like a whippy periscope to reach the somewhat inaccessible shoal. But I caught half-a-dozen very substantial Chevesnes in the next half hour. Chevesnes, which I take to be chub, are not game fish and are omnivorous (though shy) by reputation. They certainly rose freely to Greenwell and, with some around three pounds or so, it was a lot of fun. When the locals dropped their rods to see what strange foreign lure was proving so successful, it was quite an honour to introduce them to 'la Gloire de Greenwell'. If travellers in Roussillon and the Corbillère should find a modest export business for Hardy flourishing in the land of rollers, hoopoes and bee-eaters, this is the reason why.

I only hope that Greenwell will not turn in his grave at the peculiar misuse of his great invention.

Sun Perch

In the South of France some people can swim and lie in the sun all day. It's fine for two or three days, but after that there are a few males, of whom I am one, who just can't take it any more. One must do something, and the heat makes most activities almost impossible. Drawing and painting in the shade is fun, but if you are a fisherman, the time comes when the old tickling of the blood becomes irresistible. I had insisted, fortunately, on bringing my rod and my fly fishing equipment just in case, and with it I tried the sea.

Stripping a fly I threaded mussels on the hook and cast from the rocks into the deep. At the expense of massive sunburn I managed to catch a few little fellows like angel fish: pretty, bony and hardly very exciting, except for the fact that you never quite knew whether it would be a squid or a mullet next time. Failing to hook any unexpected monsters, I transferred my attention to the hills. There are mountain streams which are supposed to hold trout, and I walked for miles in the midday heat to locate them. Water snakes, gorgeous green frogs and a marvellous variety of bird and insect life, but only a couple of small trout, and one or two dead ones seen by the bank were all that I found. I gather from this that the whole population descends on reasonable rivers in the first few weeks of the season with every device known to man, legal or illegal. Anything which survives passes out in the midday heat, or retires to shady corners of the faster and more remote streams, so that throughout August nothing stirs.

Apart from a marvellous thirst and a deep tan there was little to boast of. However, I returned to my tent near the River Argens to see an angler coming back from the bank of the river across the vineyard. I intercepted him and he was proud to show me a basket full of large chub and curious fish like a cross between angel fish and perch; dark, striped and with a beautiful sheen on their scales. One of the chub was fully 5lbs—if, indeed, chub it was. I asked him if he would give me a demonstration and he was kind enough to come back on the next evening and show me how.

It was a curious proceeding. To the whistling of bee-eaters we made our way down across the vineyards past the great spotted cuckoos and the picturesque old walls to a part of the river where the steep bank is lined by clumps of bamboo through which there are little ways down to the water. The Argens is filthy, and it is hard to believe that any self-respecting fish survive, especially as it is obviously hard fished throughout the season. Nevertheless there were substantial swirls and displays on the surface.

My friend balanced himself on a ledge above the water to put out ground bait. He threaded a quaint mixture of large maggots and cheese spread and successfully cast this quite a long way out, floating it down to the bankside eddies some way downstream. Thereafter, he proceeded to haul the perch in right, left and centre.

The next night was my last. I was on my own this

time. The river had risen and I went down in breathless expectation. The ledge was only just above water level and as I cast for the first time the ledge crumbled. I went straight into the stinking water which was extremely deep. I half swam, half waded back to the shore with yellow mud of perilously impure origins up to my chest. I just rescued my rod, but not my bait, nor my hooks.

My first sun perch has yet to be caught. By I'll be back another year. At least it's cool down by the river.

Another Paradise Lost

The Valley of the Ahr used to be lovely: perhaps the nearest completely different scenery that the Continent offers to British country lovers in search of change.

This tributary of the Rhine cuts its narrow and winding way through the southern part of the Eifel, well north of the Mosel. It has much to commend it apart from its unexpected beauty: it produces an excellent light red wine; it is not on the way to anywhere in particular; and it used to be a first-class trout and grayling stream of real character.

The wine is still there. The little town of Ahrweiler near the confluence of Ahr and Rhine has vast cellars full of bins, barrels and tanks. The British do not seem to drink the Ahr wine; perhaps it does not travel well. Anyway, Germany is not famed for its red wines; this one is delicious but rather a freak. No other European red wine is produced from vineyards so far to the north. The reason is that in this valley most hilly slopes are the south-facing ones, and that the steep vineyards are grown on terraces of slate. These slates, almost without soil, present a flat surface to the midday sun and seem both to reflect and to keep the heat. The afternoon temperature in the vineyards gives an illusion of

Provence. The tops of the hills and the little tributary valleys between are, in September and October, covered with a richness of vermilion berried rowans, which are the glory of the strange Eifel landscape with its old volcanic craters, now circular lakes in a woodland setting.

Where the valley opens out towards the Rhine there is the famous inn 'Zum Sänger'. In my father's day, mine host, who had a magnificent tenor voice, attracted custom by singing Schubert. He is long since dead, but the inn still has a great and fully justified reputation. Further up the valley where the road is cramped up against the river by the steepness of the hills there is another cheerful little pub: 'die bunte Kuh' (the gaily coloured cow). It was in this stretch of the river that the best fishing used to be. I stayed at a small chalet nestling in the hilltops behind the pub. An elderly couple provided an inexpensive bed and breakfast. They had a little swimming bath and a vineyard of their own. For ornithologists there was always something to look at: rock buntings and a pair of hobbies hawking like giant swifts for insects.

The great excitement lay in the river itself, which apart from dippers, kingfishers and grey wagtails, is in total effect unlike any British streams. Yet parts of it kept reminding me of other fishing. It was full of trout and grayling in roughly equal quantities: nothing very big, but lots of well-fed sporting fish of around half-a-pound. The water was gin clear, suffering none of that slate discolouration which spoils so many of the alpine streams. Most of the river bed consisted of big bleached pebbles and stones, but here and there the slate rock of the hills plunged straight into the deeper pools. It flowed fast as a Highland burn for a hundred yards or so, but would slow down when the banks flattened out into a meadow, offering an occasional pool that was more sluggish or even muddy-bottomed. The banks offered every variety: cliffs, grass, pebble and gorse, rowan and larch woods, tangles of vine. The feeding must have been lush, for there was certainly no shortage of insects. Some of the fishing was fiendishly difficult, at other places it was delightfully easy. In size it was not unlike the upper reaches of one of the Yorkshire dale rivers or the Orchy well above Dalmally: between a big burn and a little river. The grayling dimpled the water freely on either side of the rough, where the runs at the top of the pools began to quieten down; the trout seemed to favour the more pebbly runs and rose more boldly and splashingly. Neither trout nor grayling were particular: they rose to dry flies and wet, and showed no preference for borrowed German flies over Greenwells, March Browns or Blue Duns. The Ahr in those days was neither expensive nor overfished, and if the valley even then was appreciated by tourists it was no more than an occasional bus emptying its passengers rather noisily on the 'bunte Kuh'.

All that has changed. The last time I went up the Ahr valley there were bus-loads of trippers from the Rhine valley nose to tail all along the road. It was almost impossible to get a drink, and there were vulgar little bungalows where the banks had been wild and tangled. Worst of all, although the weather had been sunny and dry for some days, the water itself was completely opaque, the colour of mushroom soup. The banks were littered with rubbish. I made enquiries and heard that a factory in a village further up was responsible. There might be a few trout in the top reaches, but there were none here; the pollution was quite deadly.

Perhaps it is not irreversible. A few years ago the Rhine itself was Europe's most vicious sewer, and it was so full of chemicals no-one would dream of bathing or even wading in it in case some effluent would make his skin or flesh rot away. The vegetation along the banks was completely decayed. The new Rhine drainage schemes are primarily aimed at containing the danger of flood, but certainly the pollution is a little less bad, though there are still very few fish tough enough to survive. Germany has not got all that many trout streams, and those that are left are becoming privately owned or very expensive. I hope she will make an effort to reclaim the Ahr: it is worth rescuing.

You don't associate the Ruhr district with trout fishing. Indeed the lower reaches of the river are no less polluted than the Rhine. But above the great towns of Hagen, Duisburg and Essen the hills above the Valley of the Wupper are as unspoilt as the Peak District and not unlike it.

Some years ago a wealthy West German industrialist was kind enough to give me a day's fishing on his strip of the Upper Wupper. He had a lovely house which contained all mod cons and blended into the landscape, and he was a splendid host.

When we set out, he offered to fix me up with a rod and equipment but I had brought my own 8ft 6in. dry fly rod. I asked for advice about choice of fly; he informed me that he always used a worm. To my surprise he produced a 12ft pole without any sophisticated equipment. In a man so vastly wealthy I had expected all the resources of German technology to produce arrays of multi-purpose fully automatic reels and ingenious lures. In fact his technique proved to be

perfectly simple: he fished upstream, wading quietly and
bent low over the water. With his long rod he just
dangled the worm into the best backwaters and eddies
and jerked the trout out.

After I had watched him catch several very small
trout, I wished him 'Petri heil!' which is the greeting
exchanged by all the German fishing fraternity, and
walked half-a-mile downstream to give him a clear run.
It was a lovely little stream not unlike the Don in its
higher reaches, a little overgrown by trees, but with
plenty of pools into which it was possible to do some
unhurried orthodox casting. Clear, clean water and
delightful, rippling, pebbly three-foot depth. Dry fly
first, for it was a fairly bright day and warm, and there
were a few Duns floating down the water. I caught some
and had a lot of fun, but they were very small and I put
them all back. A change to wet fly upstream brought me
rather more fish, but still only one or two of 10in.; most
were not more than 4in. to 7in. long. After about three
hours of this I had kept only two, but it was time to
meet my host. I feared that he would have done a great
deal better, assuming that the bigger trout must be
lurking in spots known only to him.

When I rejoined him he was cheerfully patting a very
full fishing bag. As he didn't volunteer to show them to
me I thought it more polite to conceal my curiosity. He
was obviously surprised that I should only have caught
two. We trudged back to be greeted by his blonde wife
who told us to bring the catch to the kitchen, where,
somewhat shamefaced, I produced my two.

The industrialist had indeed caught plenty: some
twenty or more—largest 8in., most 5in. or 6in. I hid my
surprise and complimented him as he obviously expected. Any critical feelings I might have had were

banished by a bottle of Graacher Goldwingert and the prospect of a dinner to match the excellent breakfast to which I had already been treated under sunshades on his terrace.

We started with hors d'oeuvres and then moved on to the trout. They were thrown complete into a deep frying pan and served like whitebait with lemon and a kind of tartar sauce. They were fried crisp and bent into hoops and crescents. It was by, British standards, baby snatching of the worst kind. One might think even at only 6in. or less that it was not very pleasant to fry trout uncleaned, but the insides came away neatly from the best fish, and they were utterly delicious. It could hardly be described as the Noble Art of game fishing: I didn't quite gather the courage to ask him why he didn't either stock with bigger trout or return the smaller ones to the water. It would have been an insult to his wife's cooking, and I have certainly never eaten better.

Waders Do Have Their Uses

I was nearly fifty years old before I was persuaded to put
on waders: a retrograde step, a foolish concession to
family pressure inspired more by deskbound softness
and increasing shame at my shorts-clad corpulence than
by commonsense.

'Wading in the water is not only an agreeable thing in
itself, but absolutely necessary in some rivers in the
North,' says William Scrope in his *Days and Nights of
Salmon Fishing.* Clearly he does not bother with waders,
for he goes on to say: 'Cut some holes in the upper
leathers of your shoes to give the water a free passage out
of them when you are on dry land . . . to prevent the
pumping noise you would otherwise make at every
step.' It is not the cold that troubles him, for he
concludes that 'in frosty weather . . . as you are likely
not to take a just estimate of the cold in the excitement of
the sport, should you be of delicate temperament and be
wading in the month of February, when it may chance
to freeze very hard, pull down your stockings and
examine your legs. Should they be black, or even purple,
it might perhaps, be as well to get to dry land, but if they
are only rubicund, you may continue to enjoy the water,
if it so pleases you.'

I've never reached the black stage, although I have

waded in shorts and gym shoes in frosty weather until I have reached a patchy purple. I might, nevertheless, draw the line at protracted wading in a cold February. What is certain is that one soon becomes accustomed to bare legs in the water; that gym shoes are safer than either thigh or breast waders and that there is no evidence that wading in cold water is bad for the health.

William Scrope is absolutely right about one's awareness of cold being lulled by the excitement of the sport. I have often been near giving up on Tweed or Don in April, frozen to the marrow, when a rise of trout has made me forget it all. I don't know whether the rush of adrenalin actually stimulates the circulation to return to numb extremities, or whether the mind is so focused on the thrill of the chase that it can register no other sensation.

In the summer months British waters are never unpleasantly cold; it is the wind and the rain which chill anglers, and the water itself is positively a refuge from the blast. I make one reservation: if you have fallen in or soaked yourself around the stomach, you may get chilled on an unpleasant day. Anglers are either fallers-in by nature, or not: I am.

I cannot resist going over the top of waders. The confounded things always leak anyway. Trout rise best in about 3ft of water, so if you are fishing dry fly upstream in a big river, you may need to be in 3ft of water yourself. If you are a wild and temperamental fisherman in a stream full of large and slippery boulders, you cannot chase those choice fat trout just beyond reach without periodically lurching in the strong current. When you have once shipped a little water, you might as well go the whole hog. The water inside soon gets warmer than the water outside.

It is wiser, too, not to waste time clambering ashore in order to hoist one loaded leg after another on to a high rock, a painful and undignified process in which quarts of water pour out all over your most intimate parts, and passers by wonder exactly what you are doing. It would, in any case, be only a few minutes before your waders were full again. Perhaps breast waders would solve the problem, but if the wearer should lose his footing they can be a death trap. In my heart of hearts I know that I should merely be tempted further in until only my head and rod would protrude, like conning tower and periscope, above the swirling waters.

The strongest argument against both thigh and breast waders is the danger they create. I never heard of a Scot who had died of cold when fishing, but I know of a number who have been drowned in Tweed or Spey after slipping in waders. The great hobnailed boots which are supposed to grip the rocks are insensitive and slippery, and the dead weight of full thigh waders makes swimming impossible.

Once you have overbalanced in a strong current you are clumsy and vulnerable. You may drop your rod and net to save yourself (though most true anglers would risk drowning first) but you can hit your head on the rocks or you can be swept out of your depth. Most dangerous of all, you can be trapped by wading out down a strong stream along a long shallow tongue with deeper waters on either side. You may find that the water rises abruptly, and that you are faced with a five-minute struggle against the current, the increasing strength of which you had not noticed, in order to regain firm ground. Many experienced fishermen have been caught this way, and some of them have lost their lives.

In shorts, woollen stockings and gym shoes life is admittedly colder, but far safer. Feet in gym shoes are sensitive to the slope of the river bed. Above all there is no danger if you fall; you are manoeuvrable, you can swim, you can twist and turn quickly, you can recover a dropped rod or net. If you should be swept out of your depth you just swim with the current until you are back in your depth, instead of sinking like a stone and praying that you may be able to scramble your way to safety along the bottom before you drown, while being rolled about like an unhorsed mediaeval knight in armour. And God preserve us all from all gadgets, like water-wings over breast waders.

My family had prophesied for me an arthritic old-age, pneumonia, and death from exposure. They have been wrong, and I would advise any energetic young man to save himself the price of such rubber monstrosities, heavy to walk in, tiresome to dry and generally superfluous. But if you are the other kind of angler, controlled and disciplined, who maintains his waders, and is capable of self-restraint and of taming his passions, then they may provide a comfort for ageing bones and spoiled livers. They will eliminate impulse and, to some extent, limit your sport.

I confess I've given way and accepted waders. It was not love of comfort—the pleasure of a hot bath and whisky after a day's soaking is among the greatest of sensual pleasures. It was the memory of a day when I had been forced by cold to give up when fishing the Don throughout a bleak and snowy midday. My wader-clad father said he thought the snow was stopping, and that he would have one more try. He returned to the hotel an hour after me with six trout, the heaviest 3lbs. I concede there are times when they have their uses.

The Greedy Pike—Fact and Fiction

Twenty miles or so north-west of the Broads and five miles from the sea lies one of Britain's treasures. Although a public road of the sleepier kind passes immediately alongside, the little lake—which I shall call Havenmill—could not be much more peaceful. The reed beds which extend for nearly half a mile beyond the far end hold not only the usual reed and sedge warblers, but, on occasion, bearded tits and bittern. Havenmill is drained by a small stream which, after diving under the road, meanders through Forestry Commission land. The hilly spruce woods flatten into a valley, treeless for a hundred yards on either side of the stream except for dwarf alders and marsh shrubs; a paradise for king-fishers, coypu, redpolls, siskins and above all grasshopper warblers.

A pike of over 30lbs was caught in Havenmill recently, and returned to the water. There are a fair number of big ones for a little lake. I am well aware that pike fishermen can be even bigger liars than other members of our inexact fraternity, and that for every pike caught and weighed of over 35lbs there are five legends of pike over 40lbs.

Since I fell in love with the place many years ago, I have been curious to see if I could disentangle fact from fiction, at least where the Havenmill pike were concerned. Ever since I saw a 20lb salmon caught on a stripped salmon fly hook artfully placed through a slice of orange peel, I have grown more willing to believe legend. Salmon may be less choosy than is usually thought, and cormorants may eat three times their weight in fish daily, but the pike, however long his sulking periods, takes a lot of beating for sheer indiscriminate voraciousness when he is on the feed.

Dick Bagnall Oakeley, the Norfolk naturalist, who was a neighbour, saw a dead 23-pounder in the reeds at Havenmill, choked to death on an undigested half-swallowed 7-pounder. This I accept, as I accept the stories of the moorhen and duck. After all, this is the part of the world where fly fishing for pike used to be practised and may, for all I know, still be tried out on occasion. The fly was like a West Highland dapping fly; a big fluffy bunch of feathers scuffled over the surface. It was probably meant to represent a tiny dabchick or newly hatched moorhen. I have not tried it, nor the sea-trout lures which are supposed to have been successful with pike; but I did hook a 5-pounder on a Woolworth's rod, a length of cotton and tiny worm hook which caught in a dead leaf, wobbled and gave me ten seconds' worth of heart failure. Another struck at and damaged a small wooden float which I was pulling in.

One morning in July at five o'clock, I saw a most unusual commotion in a shallow corner of the lake. Three large pike were swirling around, striking repeatedly, in a circle about 8ft in diameter. Inside the circle, huddled like sheep rounded up by savage dogs, a shoal of small roach were shimmering and panicking on the surface like large whitebait. One often sees small shoals splash briefly on the suface to escape a pike, but I have never before or since seen what appeared to be a systematic family hunt carried out so remorselessly or for so long. It might have lasted three minutes.

It was last winter, when the lake was three-quarters frozen, and I was looking disconsolately at the few open channels, wondering whether there was space to manoeuvre a spinner, that a small roach suddenly shot out of the water, fiercely pursued by a 3- of 4-pound pike. The roach fell on the black ice and went skidding and spinning along under its own impetus for several feet. All the pike got was a sore nose. After a dangerous rescue operation, I was able to poke the roach back safely into the water with the tip of my rod. It deserved to survive.

But none of the really remarkable pike meals come my way. More-or-less reliable friends have claimed to have caught pike on slices of bacon, a pork sausage and a packet of cigarettes. Possibly . . . but I couldn't help wondering why. After hearing these claims, I confess to having spent an uneasy hour or so dangling or dragging my breakfast sausage through the water. I believe it was my sense of the ridiculous, or fear of discovery, that led me to abandon the experiment.

More remarkable, in my view, was the discovery of a small round pool a mile from Havenmill. There was no appreciable inflow or outflow, and the pool, though comparatively deep, could not have been more than 20ft in diameter. A substantial pike was living in the pool, although I saw no other fish. He appeared to be surviving the summer. What is the smallest water which can hold a pike? Unless the foresters were surreptitiously feeding him, he must have survived on a diet of frogs and moorhen chicks.

But as for swans, terriers or ladies' hands dangling languorously and temptingly from a boat, I leave these to Irish reminiscences and Polish novels . . . or can any reader promote any of these legends to the realm of fact?

Dam That Stream

Most anglers have always dreamed of creating their own private fishing. If lust for private property is indeed at the root of all social evils and inequalities, this is capitalist sin at its most attractive. Lord, Thou knowest I do not require ten miles of salmon river for profit, nor do I ask for a vast new reservoir. It is not in me to ask for excess of riches, just as I would rather avoid extreme poverty. Just £20 000 a year in three-monthly instalments, plus a place of my own, where I can cast a fly in solitude in the evening. . . . Oh, all right. Not in complete solitude always. I don't mean to be selfish. I'll offer it sometimes to a son or to a friend, but it must be well hidden from the masses.

How powerful this instinct is! Watch any boy playing by a Highland burn. His first move is to create his own special pool by building a dam: to begin with, a boulder dam, but as he gets older and more ambitious, he will add pebbles and turf. Give him half a chance and it will be sandbags and concrete.

It is not an impossible ideal. Even a tiny stream may provide a pool four or five feet deep, of tennis court size. Not far from my home in North Norfolk, an enterprising neighbour has created a new lake. The little river

Glaven, two or three yards wide, emerges from heath-land to flow through his meadowy valley. Some four years ago he had a dam built, and a very lovely little lake resulted: about 400 yards long and between 25 and 100 yards wide, with a deep channel marking the original course of the stream. It attracted buttercups and yellow wagtails, Canada geese, tufted duck, sandpipers, oyster-catchers and not too many herons and cormorants. On the borders between hilly moorland and farmland, pebbly runs and muddy pools, the growth rate of the trout, as usually happens in newly-filled waters, was terrific.

I was one of a small syndicate hastily formed in the first year. It promised great things: on one of my first visits the trout averaged well over a pound. Unbeliev-ably naive, they rose at anything I placed before them, fought like demons, and were almost indecently fat and well fed.

One day I drove down for the evening rise. There had been a long hot spell, and I was really looking forward to trying dry fly on the big trout cruising on the surface. To my astonishment there was no lake, just a desolate mass of drying mud, and a stink of rotting weed. A friend told me later that he had been standing on the dam, when he noticed a substantial leak. He had watched spellbound and powerless as the leak grew to a stream and to an accelerating crumbling. Before long the whole contents of the lake were swept down the little river, trout and all. The herons must have had a Roman orgy, and for a while village lads had their wildest dreams come true as they picked up specimen trout from the most unlikely places with bamboo rods and worms. The decaying vegetation made it seem likely that the water flowing through the muddy mess might be polluted, but some big trout survived and made their way upstream into the virtually unfished feeder stream, where an end of season visit produced a couple of good brownies and a thrilling encounter with a really big one of some 4lbs, which I lost.

Now it has all started again under new management. A sound dam, a stock of fast-growing rainbow trout to add to a few large brown trout survivors, a careful financial basis with day tickets and payment for trout caught. A fine place to take a beginner: no trees in which to tangle casts, no formidable weed-beds in which to lose fish, easy banks, a certainty of success.

That's the trouble, of course. In Heaven the fishing will not be too good. It will be demanding and difficult, and just occasionally we shall catch (but more often lose!) enormous fish. For it is essential to human nature that there shall be the hope of something better round the next corner. And I suspect that sink and draw techniques will be banned. At the beginning of the season success is unlikely without such methods. Before the trout come to the surface, a whiskey, an Alexandra, a worm-fly, a double hooked bloody butcher or, indeed, any old sea-trout or mackerel feather lure will be more effective than a quickly moved wet fly near the top. Highly efficient—but how one misses the inimitable thrill of casting at a selected rising trout, of anticipating and seeing him rise and of timing one's strike. It is hard, when sinking one's fly, to get rid of the feeling that one is cheating, that one is only pretending not to be spinning. Drop your rod, have a sandwich, take a swig at the bottle, pick up your rod again, put it on your shoulder and walk four or five yards along the bank, and you are just as likely to catch a fish (even if it should only be a pikelet!) as your neighbour who is concentrat-

ing on imparting lively movement to the fly, obeying all
the rules and has every nerve tingling for quick response.

But this is very ungracious. The venture has been an
unqualified success. There must be scope for others to
follow my neighbour's example. There is no shortage of
small streams, there are efficient fish farms, there is
much good advice available, and there are stretches of
water with suitable and little used banks. In times when
meat and fish are costly, Norfolk trout could become as
great an asset to our tables as Norfolk turkey, as well as
providing one of the county's most attractive sports. In
the unlikely event of there being a glut of trout, perhaps
some super salesman will have the energy to convert the
English to the same appreciation and love of carp which
has, for years, been the preferred Christmas treat of the
Germans and the Poles.

In the meantime I'm still looking for a streamlet and a
site for one more private and personal tennis court-sized
pool, not for sale, not for hire, not for you . . . but for
me. And for someone who really knows how to make a
small dam foolproof.

The Major's Pool

The Major's pool is an awesome place. The river here winds its way in a horseshoe through wooded hills; its banks are three hundred feet high, steep enough to offer only a precarious foothold for the glorious beeches which colour them like bracken in October. At the other end of the year, in April, there is a carpet of primroses in the mossy patches between rocks.

The river echoes the changing moods of its banks. Between fifty and one hundred yards wide, its bed produces some of the most dangerous wading in Britain. A few feet above the water, a crumbling path winds along the bottom of the gorge. Slippery, shelving rocks alternate with big boulders which, in high summer, are made more treacherous by slime. Above the Major's pool there is half a mile or more of lovely trouting water. The edges are overhung by trees, and the depth varies deceptively between two and five feet, with a few deeper parts, where the powerful, swirling main stream slows down momentarily into half pools. In dry weather it is all quite friendly; but thunderstorms can raise the level by feet in a matter of minutes. The colour then thickens from beer to ruddy mud, and mangolds, branches, whiskey bottles, even trees and drowned sheep are swept down into the pool. At the bottom of the trout water, the river broadens, accelerates smoothly and dizzily, and then narrows again into a hundred yards of turbulent rapids and jagged rocks.

There is one brief pause for a half pool where the sea-trout rest behind a great central boulder, and then the river pours and thunders into the Major's pool. The current has eaten away the far bank here and it runs deep and black below the steepest part of the hill. Halfway down, where the broken water begins to smooth, the salmon lie. At the head and tail of the 300 yards pool, the trout favour three or four feet of water, where the shallows of the river bank shelve down towards the depths of the main stream.

From the first wintry days of the salmon season to its autumnal end, the small determined figure of the Major could be seen thrashing the water from top to bottom and back again. Never has there been so dedicated a fisherman: salmon, sea-trout and brown trout, wet fly or dry. I never met him anywhere but in the water. I don't suppose many people did in the last few years. Once he had retired from the army, he didn't miss a day of the season, except Sundays. He was first at the water and last to leave it. Undeterred by hail, snow, gales or drought, he knew every stone, every backwater, every run and ripple of that two mile stretch.

An unusual looking man: grey-haired and rather small, though well-built; his face was not surprisingly weathered, like a Highland ghillie's, to a rich purple, but he had big, brown sad eyes in place of the more characteristic fisherman's blue. From casual conversations over a picnic lunch on the great slanting rocks at the head of the pool, I knew that he was a good ornithologist: he loved the flashing goosanders, the primrose yellow of the grey wagtails, the busy dippers and the dapper oystercatchers which kept us company. Rumour had it that he had been quite a lady's man and even a poet. He had evidently left the army because he had found peace-time soldiering an empty social round with companions who had bored him. But things had gone wrong: a broken marriage: a failed business venture; an expensive mistress with a fear of raw countryside and a dislike of fishing, who eventually left him for a younger man. He was now tired of society and none too fit, and he did little else but fish.

In the off season he disappeared, nobody knew where. He still had some money, and it was conjectured that he holidayed abroad, restlessly whiling away the time in successive hotels, watching birds, tying flies and dreaming of the time when he would renew his assault on the luckless fish.

Last April he was back as usual. The first warm days after the snow was out of the water brought some marvellous rises of trout early in the afternoon. The Major forsook his salmon rod and made his way up the tricky little path to the head of the trout water. The clouds chased across the sun; showers, dancing light and glare alternating with shadows and scudding ripples. He was sixty, and the walk in heavy waders was hot and wearying work. A glance at a favourite backwater told him all he needed to know. Wind downstream, water a little high and coloured, and no real hatch of fly yet. He would try downstream wet.

He lowered himself painfully into the water, swearing to himself as his net caught in a bramble. Using a landing net as a third leg, he groped his way out carefully, until he was far enough out to be clear of the overhanging trees. It was as well that he was so experienced; the weight of the water made it a real effort not to lose ground downstream at every stride, and it pushed heavily at the back of his knees. How often he had slipped, banged himself painfully, dropped rod or net, shipped gallons of water into his waders, performed grotesque dances to save himself from being swept downstream, spent the rest of the day cold and wet. Once on shore he would be forced to lift his legs alternately and indecorously onto a high rock to empty the contents of each wader—as much onto the more intimate portions of his anatomy as onto the bank.

He started to cast, beautifully as ever. He was incapable of a bad cast in any conditions or in any style; whether down or upwind, right or left-handed, back-handed or speyside. The flies, wet or dry, always landed lightly and in line, without splash or drag. Gusts or overhanging trees which put others in a tangle just summoned up more reserves of artistry and ingenuity from the Major. Soon he hooked a good fish at the very extremity of a long line. In the powerful current it fought like a 3-pounder, and he nearly lost it when he staggered on a slimy boulder and the rod jerked; he landed it, however. The rain started again; the swift sliding of the water and the strain of watching his flies on the ripples made him feel strangely giddy. He was on a shallow tongue which reached out, down and across towards the main stream; the trout lay just short of the rough water. The Major saw a fly, and then another: they looked like Greenwells. Just beyond his reach, half a dozen large trout started to pick them off. The Major pulled more line off his reel, and took a couple more steps towards them. As he did so, his foot slipped a little and he shipped a mass of water over the top of his waders. Where he had been sweating with the effort of wading across the stream, he gasped at the sudden cold. His heart hammered at the strain of recovering his balance. Not a bad death really, he thought to himself, as he had thought a hundred times, and he grinned wryly to himself. Back on an even keel, he ignored the cold and his wet midriff, and took two more rather steadier steps towards the fish. But the trout were no longer rising and he noticed that the water had coloured a little. Perhaps he should get back to shore and dry out the waders. The shower was now heavy, and he was getting very cold. As he turned to short cut his way back to the bank, he found that there was a deeper channel between him and the shore. Damn, he muttered to himself: he should have remembered that little trap. Turning again upstream he tried to force his right leg to take a stride against the current. Such was the force of the water now that he could not move it without the risk of the other leg being swept from under him. To steady himself, he bent heavily on his net. The metal pole tip slipped, and he lurched, right off balance. Dropping rod and net, he grabbed at the big underwater boulder and missed. He was swept off his feet and rolled into deeper water. It'll be all right, he thought, if I can just keep my head above water enough to breathe. I'll let myself go until I'm washed into the half pool, and then I'll crawl my way into the shallows. He'd visualised it all before and had often saved himself by giving way with the current where others struggled. But the current was unexpectedly swollen and fierce; he found himself momentarily out of his depth and took in a nasty breathful of water. Choking and spluttering, he was whisked into a great rock, and the beeches and primroses of the gorge spun confusedly overhead. He felt a sharp pain in his back, and was hurled into the main stream.

With a sudden and extraordinary relief it flashed into his mind that this was it: he was too tired to fight. There were two more sickening bangs and another lungful of water, then he was rolled under again too fast even to know which way up he was—then nothing more.

That evening I found his body, washed up on the great slanting rocks at the head of his pool. The water had gone down again; I thought he was sleeping, except that a curious dipper was bobbing up and down beside him. It was, I believe, appropriate. Only the Doctor and I, and possibly the Major himself, knew that he would not in any case have had more than a few weeks to live.

In Praise of Schubert

Schubert understood water music from the dance of the mill wheels to the ruffling of a still pool by the first breeze of evening. No angler could listen to him without a thrill of recognition.

When the BBC decides to do something worthwhile, it does it well. Anniversary programmes are often a bore, but this year their efforts with Schubert have been marvellous.

I'm biased; something to do with my German grandmother, no doubt. I get uncomfortable shivers at Wagnerian music, and reach surreptitiously for my handkerchief at Schumann. A corner of me is Scottish enough to be ashamed of that; but no one need conceal unashamed delight, joy and tears, when he hears Schubert, because it is music of transparent genuineness and goodness.

Why has he been so neglected compared with Beethoven or Bach? It cannot be that we all prefer the vast and the monumental and powerful to the more brief and evanescent beauties of pure lyricism. In a cynical and sophisticated age, Schubert may seem almost naïvely emotional. Apart from two great symphonies, he provides little for the concert and opera repertoires of contemporary fashion. Vast concert halls and the mass audiences are not for him; above all composers he is intimate. His Lieder are for artists who can establish a close relationship with each member of a small audience. They do not require great overtrained voices so much as romantics of the profoundest understanding and delicacy.

That is why Wilfred Brown, for instance, was to those privileged to hear and understand him more profoundly moving in a drawing room recital than Dietrich Fischer-Dieskau. Schubert composed to entangle his friends, performers and audience in a community of joy and sorrow in a manner that thrived on physical nearness. Paradoxically television is a most effective vehicle for him. The magic box that makes all things small is powerless to reduce Schubert—it just brings him home to us in an intimate way.

Impromptus, sonatas, moments musical, trios, the *Schöne Müllerin* and the *Winterreise*—all marvellous. The height of lyricism was reached, however, in the *Trout* Quintet. It may not have the heartbreaking profundity of some of the *Winterreise* songs, or the mystery and drama of *Erlkönig*, but it has magic. However much the *Trout* theme has been done to death by the vulgarity of incurably English performers unaware of the crudity of their acts of murder, this performance of the Quintet by young and gifted soloists, recorded from rehearsal to ultimate perfection, was sheer joy . . . well on second thoughts not perfection. Performances of Schubert should never be perfect. Franz was too spontaneous and human, and his music calls for youth and abandon, even exaggeration. Despair, ebullience, bitterness, sweetness and exhilaration can be driven out of perfection, or cramped by over intelligent good tastes.

What wonderful viewing that great Quintet provided. Jacquelin Dupré at her best making her 'cello bound and quiver with her own joy. Zukerman apparently as far beyond any technical limitations as if he had been playing his normal first violin role. Opposite him the infinitely expressive and happy face of the violinist Perlman from much the same musical background as himself, responding to and conveying the tiniest whispers of mood-and-tempo-change with a similarity of musical interpretation and temperament which had to be seen to be believed. The bass player, Zubin Mehta, more often thought of as a conductor, seemed to be caught up into and held in this mysterious unity, as though in a trance.

The unity necessarily owed as much to the pianist as to anybody. In the *Trout* the piano often provides the constant movement of the water in which the other instruments sparkle and flash and ripple and tumble in turn. The pianist David Barenboim, seemed electrically aware of what everyone was doing; the ideal accompanist, never obtruding, always precise, always providing the framework on which the others could embroider, but himself embroidering and embellishing with the best as the roles exchanged.

Programme music that imitates cuckoos or thunder, and tells stories can be (forgive me, Beethoven) irritating. But the *Trout* Quintet never labours its descriptiveness. It is pure, sunlit water music; the essence of spring by the brookside. The phrases dart and trill, ebb and flow in interweaving liquid patterns: they are like eddies and swirls and bubbles, sparkling and dazzling their rhythmic way over a gleaming mosaic of pebbles. The cameras did it all justice: hands and arms, smiling lips, and raised eyebrows, bows and keys performed a ballet:

melodies and accompaniments shuttled back and forth as faces were utterly lost in the joy of recreation.

Is there anything more thrilling in music than the movement in which, towards the end, the 'cello and the bass take up the central melody slowly and peacefully against this restless onward drive of the rippling piano? Schubert understood water music from the dance of the water mills to the ruffling of a still pool by the first chill breeze of evening. No angler could listen to him without a thrill of recognition.

In his choice of poems to set to music Schubert had instictive good taste. The greatest and best poems of his time sprang to music in his mind. To this good taste there was apparently, one exception. The words of Wilhelm Müller's *Schöne Müllerin* and *Winterreise* to which Schubert wrote so many of his most beautiful melodies and accompaniments, have seemed, to many critics, sentimental, commonplace and full of cliché. I believe they miss the point.

The one great quality which lay slumbering in Müller's oversimple verse, awaiting for Schubert's touch to awaken it, was the agonised, nostalgic, bitter sweet, tragic passion for all the evanescent pleasures of life of a young man doomed to an early death.

This at once struck the deepest chord of recognition in Schubert, in whose hands the mood came alive and gained immortality. And because we are all the prisoners of a dying animal, Schubert and Müller brought the human condition home to us with a heightened force and sincerity that has never been excelled. It is this which will ensure that to sentimental amateurs like myself (who will always be in the majority), Schubert will survive all the changes of taste and fashion and keep the very special place he deserves.